MW01204434

I love and you

John

FAI✝H
L♡VE
AND
HYPN◉SIS

AN INSPIRATIONAL MEMOIR OF THE DANCE
BETWEEN STROKE AND HEALING.

JANE GAGE GOVONI

BALBOA.
PRESS
A DIVISION OF HAY HOUSE

Balboa Press books may be ordered through booksellers or by contacting:

Balboa Press
A Division of Hay House
1663 Liberty Drive
Bloomington, IN 47403
www.balboapress.com
1 (877) 407-4847

Because of the dynamic nature of the Internet, any web addresses or
links contained in this book may have changed since publication and
may no longer be valid. The views expressed in this work are solely those
of the author and do not necessarily reflect the views of the publisher,
and the publisher hereby disclaims any responsibility for them.

The author of this book does not dispense medical advice or prescribe the use
of any technique as a form of treatment for physical, emotional, or medical
problems without the advice of a physician, either directly or indirectly. The
intent of the author is only to offer information of a general nature to help
you in your quest for emotional and spiritual well-being. In the event you use
any of the information in this book for yourself, which is your constitutional
right, the author and the publisher assume no responsibility for your actions.

Any people depicted in stock imagery provided by Thinkstock are models,
and such images are being used for illustrative purposes only.
Certain stock imagery © Thinkstock.

Print information available on the last page.

ISBN: 978-1-5043-5976-4 (sc)
ISBN: 978-1-5043-5978-8 (hc)
ISBN: 978-1-5043-5977-1 (e)

Library of Congress Control Number: 2016909814

Balboa Press rev. date: 10/06/2016

I dedicate this book to those who were at the center of
my healing, the people that love me and
whom I love with all my heart.

DISCLOSURE

This is my story about how I healed from a major stroke. I am
not a doctor; I am just a person who recovered from a very rocky
path. Based on personal observations and experience, the author and
publisher expressly disclaim responsibility for any adverse effects
arising from the use or application of the information contained
in this book. Mindfulness, hypnotism and many other approaches
presented here are stand-alone and adjunct legal health-care, help-
care wellness approaches and not the exclusive domain of any
licensed healing arts profession.

TABLE OF CONTENTS

INTRODUCTION

God has given each of us our "marching orders."
Our purpose here on Earth
Is to find those orders and carry them out.
Those orders acknowledge our special gifts.

— Soren Kierkegaard

This book may appear to be my story of healing from a medical condition, but in my mind it is about resilience. At some time, we all find ourselves on a rocky road, fighting our own dragons. My dragon was named stroke. I was told, "Jane, you lost a third of your brain. The stroke was caused by a very rare brain disease. There is no cure and no treatment. So, go home and get your things in order." I was expected to die or be in a nursing home.

I needed to take my health into my own hands, but I was not alone. Just like you, I had helpers and angels, both earthly and heavenly, everywhere along my path. We are told that we have faith, hope and love, and the greatest is love. There was no medicine or surgery available for me, but there was love everywhere I turned.

If you are on your own rocky path, be it a physical, emotional, mental or spiritual challenge, I give you what worked for me. My healing recipe is a combination of humor, Eastern philosophy, modern Western medicine ideas, Native American wisdom, and the beliefs from generations of my family, all wrapped in my faith and served with a big helping of love.

Step by step, I created my healing plan with the beliefs and skills I knew. Hypnosis is my gift, and it was a very large part of my healing. When we can learn to control our own thoughts, we can create health in our bodies. My faith creates a belief in my mind that whatever happens to me, God will work to create something good.

Chapter 1

THE STORM

I was doing the dishes on the evening of August 12th 1998, when Jim came to the kitchen window and asked if I wanted to take the dogs for a walk with him. I smiled and shook my head no. Instantly, I realized I couldn't make words leave my mouth. Quickly I turned, feeling panic surging through my body. On the second step, I collapsed, hitting the edge of the stove hard enough to chip a tooth. I had the irrational thought if I could take a bath, I would feel better. I know the thought was irrational, but in my defense, my brain was shutting down. I was very definitely in fight or flight mode, and when that happens our energy goes to our arms to fight and our legs to run. Our prefrontal cortex thinking brain is not getting a lot of power. Habit takes over, and we do what we know how to do in a similar situation. My habit is to take a bath; it has always been my way to comfort myself when I feel broken. But this time I was too broken, and I realized that when I couldn't get up from the floor, so I started to crawl upstairs. When I reached the tub, I couldn't remember how to turn the water on. I crawled to my bed, pulled my quilt over me, and passed out.

My very intuitive daughter, Gina, said she heard me calling her, so she ran into the house and woke me up. By this time, I was only answering in very garbled speech. She called her dad, and in minutes he was there. When he went to the phone to dial 911, I became so agitated, pointing to my grandma's house next door. I didn't want her to be afraid. They understood, and between the two of them, they got me into the car and rushed me the 28 miles to the hospital. Jim was driving too fast, hoping to get pulled over by the police, but it felt like we were flying through a deserted world; nothing was real.

The three of us moved through the emergency doors, and I heard Jim yell, "My wife is having a stroke, please hurry!" and they did. This is the moment I became the observer of my life.

If you have ever water skied, you know if you stay right behind the boat, the water is calm. On both sides of you are rolling hills of water. I stayed in that smooth calm, watching while everyone around me was jumping the waves. I thought, "So this is what it feels like to have a stroke."

The doctor asked if I would please tell him what year it was, and I answered, "1812." Obviously a memorable year in my distant past!

My blood pressure was still not extremely elevated, even though I wanted to tell them that it was very high for me. But I didn't have the words, so I settled back into being a peaceful observer. They made arrangements to send me the 45 miles away to the University Hospital after the CAT scan proved I had a stroke.

Gina had called her sisters, and within 30 minutes the ER lobby was populated by Jim, all four girls and Maria's boyfriend, Mom, brother John, and Aunt Jan. The observer in me could feel their fear as my mother came back to see me. I was still in the eye of the storm and felt relatively calm, or as calm as you can be with all the poking and monitoring being done in an emergency room.

I could hear my brother saying over and over to anyone who would listen, "She will be sick; she gets motion sickness-please give her something before you put her in an ambulance." I really do get sick, and I have since I was a small child. Since I became 16, I drive whenever possible or sit the front seat. I am pretty sure those two options were not possible in this situation. The observer in me decided it probably was a little problem right now.

My mother came back to the exam room and I said, "scared." She thought I was scared, but I wanted her to know I didn't want her to be scared. I said it over and over to make her understand. It would be the first time, but not the last, that what I said and what I meant would not be understood. Anyone who has experienced a stroke or a brain trauma knows it is frustrating to deal with all the communication challenges. She told me that they were all praying, and she knew it would be okay. I smiled and focused on Jim's hand over mine as I slid in and out of reality.

I woke up in the ER of the University of Wisconsin Hospital waiting for something. There was an IV in my arm, filling me with cold from the inside out, like tiny crushed ice pushing through my veins. I could hear the sounds of ambulances as they arrived and people running and calling to each other. It was a hot August night, and I felt as if I was freezing. A nurse stopped by and told me that there had been a bad accident, but I would be taken to a room soon. She noticed that I was shivering and got me a blanket from the warmer, and it felt wonderful. I slid back and forth from one reality to what felt like a deep sleep. Thoughts and feelings bubbled up and swirled like I was on the inside of a lava lamp. Although it was as easy for me to make myself understood as a lava lamp, I still had thoughts.

I wondered where Jim was and hoped he wasn't part of the accident. I would feel warmer if he was here. Where was Jim? I needed to feel his hand if I was to stay rooted to the earth. It was getting harder and harder to stay in the calm. I closed my eyes and slid away.

I awoke in a room, and the only question I could answer when asked, was my name was Jane. I heard someone in the hall say, "I am looking for my wife, Govoni." I thought, "That sounds familiar, maybe that is my name." A second later I heard, "I am looking for my sister, Gage," and I thought, "That sounds familiar, maybe that is my name." Then two men walked in, my husband and my brother, and I knew them as I would know everyone I loved.

Jim came over and asked what I needed; should he stay or go home to the girls? Then he said, "We can do this; you are going to be all right." He pulled me back to earth and secured me with those simple words. He leaned over, kissed me, and went home. I think anyone we live with for a long time gets to feel our feelings rather than listen to our words. My brother John stayed.

Big Medicine

This is my favorite poem, but it is written by an unknown poet, and that is too bad, because I wish I could tell this wise person that these words were big medicine for me. Bigger than anything modern medicine had to offer, as I came to my edge of light.

When you come to the edge of all the light you have known,

And are about to step off into the darkness of the unknown,

Faith is knowing one of two things will happen,

There will be something solid to stand on or

You will be taught to fly.

> "Why, sometimes I've believed as many as six
> impossible things before breakfast."
> **– Lewis Carroll**

I believed that if I took care of my body, and was kind to others, life would be kind to me. This is much too simple. I now believe we should not only take care of our body and be kind, but also that life is magical, and it has a much better plan than we can imagine. And that magical plan life has for us, is how we are taught to fly.

Our lives are many chapters long, and when I was 46 years old, I started the second half of my life. In fact, the second half of my life started on August 12, 1998.

Recap of the first 45 years before the storm in a nutshell

If you were reading "The Book of Jane," you may remember the first part ends with more stress than was normal for our character. My dad had died in the last year, and that felt like an earthquake and had knocked the foundations of my world off balance. Our oldest daughter, Becca, had been very sick, and she had a number of surgeries. Becca was graduating from college and getting married in November. Maria, our second daughter, was in college. Our third daughter, Amanda, was leaving for college, and our last child, Gina, was a junior in high school. I no longer knew my place in life. Everything was changing.

Mothering had been such a large part of my happiness that it had long feelers into every part of my being. It wasn't just these four beautiful, intelligent woman that I loved; I also truly enjoyed their friends and loved to hear the idealism and passion that those young people expressed. This part of my life was coming to an end, and deep inside I felt a restlessness starting to grow. Inside I watched those bubbles in the pot of feelings getting ready to break into a boil. You could hear, if you really listened, to a deep inner spirit asking, "Who will you be when your job is finished?" I would answer, "Ridiculous! I will be who I have always been; I will be a wife, a mother, a coach and a hypnotist." The empty nest is real; there is a deep fear inside that you are not the same person you were with kids, and you can't be the person you were before kids.

The empty nest isn't really about kids; it could be about a job you loved, a divorce, a financial loss, or a severe illness. The empty nest is really that never-comfortable place of what is no longer and what is not yet.

For a few months, I was troubled because I could hear my blood pounding in my head; there was no pain but a pounding that I could not escape. Walking up the stairs became an effort, because it felt like my energy was leaking out of my body. "Tired" is a little word, and it alone couldn't explain my feeling exhausted and fatigued. No, words were all too lightweight. I was weary, but it was the noise that was driving me to distraction, the sounds of my blood pounding through the arteries of my head.

When I became so dizzy that the world turned upside down, I knew something was seriously wrong. All I could do was hold on. The dizziness was like a ride at an amusement park. You know the one that you must be 48 inches tall to ride, and then you can strap yourself in as you go back and forth and spin around and upside down. Yes, that dizzy.

The doctor checked my blood pressure, which was good; it was higher than my normal 105/70, but normal for a warm-blooded human. There was a virus that was going around: worry-stress-change of life-premenopausal-blah, blah, blah.

Stress is not all bad; I mean there is good stress, called eustress, that keeps us motivated and moving. We will have stress until we are in a pine box and people are saying, "Doesn't she look nice." It is when we stay in a constant stress mode, our body in a fight / flight mode, and our endocrine system going crazy, that we are in trouble. This causes distress, and this stress is the cause of 94% of all doctor visits. In fact, the NIH (National Institute of Health) says that 85-90% of all illness is stress-related.

So it was very logical that someone who had seldom even had the flu was just experiencing a virus or symptoms of stress. The spinning stopped after a few hours; I think my body was just trying to get my attention. One change after another was happening. I am normally a half-full kind of person. My journals were another hint that something was very wrong.

Journals

January 3rd 1998
Rachel called today and said she was going to be a grandma and she felt old. I don't feel old and I don't feel young, actually most of the time I don't feel. I don't feel any more real than the characters in my books. I am moving through life as an observer but most of the time I dread being observed. I don't want anyone to see who I am or what I think. I am changing so fast becoming withdrawn from life, maybe I have always been an introvert in an extrovert's body. I no longer have the energy to cover it up. At one time I knew who I was, I believed I knew who God was and what he demanded of me. I am no longer so innocent and although I still believe in God, I don't pretend to know what he is thinking about, or if he is thinking about me at all.

March 8th 1998

Gina was confirmed today. Jill and Ken came in a snowstorm. Pastor Paul confirmed her. I have a big thing off my to do list. I have provided the base. I hope they will now all find their spiritual path. It is harder and harder to think of my life as a group activity. Am I progressing to another stage or regressing? Jim is so grounded and I feel a strong wind could blow me away, farther and farther like Dorothy to the land of Oz. Amanda will graduate in a couple months and Gina not far behind. Becca and Eric have decided to get married, Maria is away in college. My house, my life, I am changing so fast, I dread Jim and I moving through this big old house alone but I no longer have the energy or patience to have them all here. This is becoming so hard; I am so tired I must be at a leaping off point. I am thankful and love my life and yet at the same time dissatisfaction is gnawing, eating me inside.

When you enter what the Christian mystic St. John of the Cross called the "dark night of the soul," you are unable to see the gifts hidden in the pain. It has been described as a time when the spark of our spirit flickers and burns weakly. For me, I felt lost, and I felt like my face was being pushed into the mud. Every time I got up, I was pushed down harder, further down where my heart beat louder and louder. I wondered why people couldn't hear the beating. Why couldn't Jim hear it in the quiet of the night, when he was right next to me?

The Talmud tells us there is always a gift hidden among the pain. So we are told to say, "Thank you" to everything that happens, even before we know what the gift will be. I was finding very little about my health to be happy about.

Maybe Kierkegaard said it best when he wrote, "Life can only be understood backwards; but it must be lived forwards." I lived forward, and I did what I was trained to do. First by my mother, who had always told us we would feel better if we washed our face, brushed our teeth and combed our hair. I think if we checked our genealogy, our mother may have the same DNA as the 18th century novelist, Laurence Sterne, who said about his character, Tristram Shandy, when he felt sluggish and stupid, he would change into his best shirt and coat, put on his topaz ring and his finest 18th century powdered wig, "A man cannot dress, but his ideas get clothed at the same time."

Hypnotists talk about faking it until you make it, and science knows that our body affects our mind, and our mind affects our body. It is why we can think of something embarrassing and we blush. Our thoughts create a biochemical reaction.

I would smile and act as normal as possible, doing everything short of putting on a powdered wig. Then, I would make sure the brick wall that held my fear tightly confined had all the bricks firmly in place. If I would have been my own client, I would have asked myself how long I thought I could hold that beach ball under water. Our feelings are like a beach ball; if we are healthy and resilient, we can bounce and be light. However, none of us are able to hold that ball under water very long before it escapes our grasp.

It was part of my daily routine to imagine breathing in pure oxygen from my big old willow tree in the back yard, filling myself with energy. One day, one of the girls saw me hugging that big willow. She laughed and asked what I was doing. I smiled back and said, "You know I am a tree hugger." I could imagine that old tree sharing her energy with me.

> *"What's in a name? That which we call a rose by*
> *any other name would smell as sweet."*
> **– Hamlet/ Shakespeare**

Names

Names are a funny thing, especially for women. I never really felt like a Govoni, and yet it had been a long time since I was a Gage. I was "Jane," and even that was a name given to me before anyone knew me. We are given nicknames by friends who may see a different side to our personality, but in this culture our names identify us like a tag on our chest. In many cultures it is very different. You may be given a birth name, but you will be given a name that speaks of your actions. When I was a young woman, I chose to study the Native Americans in my area, the Ho-Chunk people. My father told me that his grandma was Ho- Chunk, and he was raised in a way that was very close to nature. He looked very much like a Native American. This interested me, and I plagued my Native American friend that ran her family's Indian Museum with question after question, until she passed me off to an "uncle," and this very, very patient man became my tutor. One day after many months, he told me I was to get a new name; I was Little Wave Maker. It was very appropriate for me, because I have a tendency to question things, which tends to make waves.

A few years later, my mom and I were driving through some hills on a very beautiful day when she looked at me and said, "If you would have been born in the 60's rather than the 50's, I would not have named you Jane. I would have named you Sky, Sky Blue." Of course I asked her why, and she said, "Because I think it fits you better than Jane." She was finished with the conversation, but a new conversation started in my head. "Sky" felt right in a way that "Jane" never had. However, unless I moved across country and made new relationships, it would be quite difficult to get everyone on board to think of me in this new way. So I created my business as "Sky Blue Dreams." My business would become my dream and in my head I would be "Sky Blue." Maybe W.C. Fields was right when he said, "It ain't what they call you, it's what you answer to that matters."

I believe that there are two pieces to each of us; there is the ego and the soul. My ego is Jane. Ego often gets a bad rap, but we need that part of us to get up and create our life in the world we live in. Ego has a hard job, because some of the pieces of our personality that it has to deal with are fear and competition. Your Soul, or your best self, deals with love and compassion. Jane deals with one side of my reality, but many times a day I ask, "What would Sky say about this?"

The Hospital

Now we started with the tests. This is what was written on my chart:

Garbled speech--confused and restless, asks in a slow manner, "Will I get better? Has to go fast. Don't know why this?"

PT. knows her first name. When asked the month she answered, "Alaska," rather than, "August." Has no idea what a clock, calendar or money is, and is unable to repeat words or phrases. She uses gestures to respond. Patient is cooperative.

I walked into the bathroom, and as I was ready to leave, I saw the roll of toilet paper. I remember thinking, "This is important." I stood there a minute, unrolled some paper and threw it into the waste basket.

Later charts:

The news is too difficult for her to follow. Can retrieve 4 words for a sentence, has asked for more practice words. Pt. seems relaxed and happy with her improvement. Carotid dissection - light touch sensory loss in both upper and lower extremities. MRI - L interior carotid completely Blocked - R interior carotid occluded with dissection. She has followed 1-step directions with required motor responses. 1 out of 8 correct, oral/verbal apraxia - difficulties with comprehension, word retrieval and written language - very motivated patient.PT. brother present and has practiced pronunciation of family member's names, months, numbers etc.

My brother John is seventeen years younger than I am, and he stayed next to my bed, his 6-foot-three-inch frame folded into the chair. He always seemed to be awake when I opened my eyes, and he always had yet another question for me. I was very happy if he didn't see me open my eyes! Whenever the doctors, nurses or any therapist came in, he listened and collected a whole set of new questions. One day a doctor came in and pulled some change from his pocket and asked me what it was. I had absolutely no clue. He gave me the change and told me to hold it, hoping that it would start the connection process. I was grateful for the shiny gift, but it stirred little interest in me. John was very interested in this new set of questions. Now when I opened my eyes, we talked about time, clocks, and money - all very foreign concepts to me.

While most stroke patients receive a short therapy session every day, I had 24-hour therapy. One night, John woke me up, because a medical helicopter landed on the roof outside of my room. This opened up a completely new avenue of things of which I had no memory. We all have forgotten a name or an answer, and we feel it is right on the tip of our tongue, but this is different. After a brain injury, there is a black wall. I had no illusion that I was going to remember. "Poof!" it had disappeared. Elvis had left the building; it was that kind of gone. Still, there was the feeling that I was expected to understand what people were talking about.

Prognosis

One day my brother went home to shower and rest, because my friend Janie had agreed to stay in the room at all times and write down anything I was told to do. We were trying to chat, but mostly we were just sitting in that companionable silence that you understand if you have a friend that you have had for many years. An intern came in with some charts and pictures. He started talking and always asked if I understood. This is what I understood:

1. You have had a stroke, because you have a rare brain disease called hyper-fibro-dysplasia.
2. The linings of your carotid arteries and other arteries in your brain have collapsed. Everywhere they collapsed you have many clots.
3. You lost a third of your brain due to the stoke.
4. If you live, which we don't expect, it will be in a nursing home.
5. There is no medical treatment for this disease.
6. You should get your affairs in order.

I was pretty sure he had flunked bedside manner, and now I was seeing two of him, and both of him had started to speak a foreign language. So, before he could ask if I understood again, I closed my eyes and slipped into sleep. My mind needed to sort out its own truth.

First of all, I understood death. We were all going to die, the question was not if, but when, and it seemed to me that if the Good Lord wanted me to die, that is what would happen. I really had absolutely no fear about dying. I had a brother die as an 8-month-old baby when I was two years old, and my father had just died. We all see people die; it is a natural part of life. I believed there was a very good chance I would die.

I had prime real estate on the hospital floor, right across from the nurses' station. I was monitored constantly, and that was a very good sign that this was pretty serious. But a nursing home - that almost made me laugh, that was ridiculous to my brain, body and spirit. Death was not a great threat; I would be with God and my dad; I knew and loved many people on the other side. It was the ultimate travel experience. I had not planned on taking that trip right now, but God would deal with that.

But that young, clumsy doctor was mistaken about a nursing home, because that was nowhere on my travel list. My brain believed that if the doctor was wrong about this, then the whole prognosis could be wrong. Our brain does not like incongruent ideas, and usually that is what creates stress in our body. We have the desire to do one thing, but we think we should do something else - incongruent idea - so the result is stress.

But for some reason, this did not cause me stress. This young intern was my greatest helper, because I heard his words like a dare rather than a death sentence. Even as a child, if I perceived a dare, there was something inside of me that would do anything to find a way to go over, under, around or through the challenge. Someone told me that this was because I am an Aries, and it was the Ram in me. The fact was, I had experienced a stroke.

Here are a few stroke statistics from the American Heart Association:

1. Stroke is the third leading cause of death in the United States, and the leading cause of disability.
2. Stroke kills about 150,000 Americans a year, or 1 out of three stroke victims.
3. Strokes affect men more often than women, although women are more likely to die from a stroke.

4. Two-thirds of strokes occur in people over the age of 65.
5. Stoke affect blacks more than whites.
6. 10% of stroke victims recover almost completely, with minor impairments

Our Brain is often compared to a computer, and using this analogy, it is as if my computer crashed that August evening. The difference is, when you need a new computer, the computer technician/ magician can transfer all of your old documents in the memory of your old drive and "voila," you are as good as new. Had this situation been a computer, the right people would be put in place with the right programs. But with my situation, there were no programs, no prescriptions, no written medical plan, and there was no team of physicians. Had this been a computer, it would have surely been thrown away. Clearly, the human brain is more complicated. It was the human spirit from inside me that continued to focus on ways to resolve my situation and connect me again with the divine to create a plan that could heal my life.

*Chapter 2*

THE COUNCIL

Napoleon Hill has been one of the people whose work I have studied and loved. He wrote the best self-help book of all time, "Think and Grow Rich," in 1937, and it is still loved today. Napoleon talks about creating a board of directors that can advise you as you make life's decisions. The first time I read that, I totally understood it, because when I was in my twenties I had a dream. I was trying to find a mistake in my account book, and I was having a tough time of it. It seemed as if no matter how many times I added each column, I got the same numbers, and I was $100 dollars off.

That night I dreamt that I walked into a room with a long table and quite a few black leather chairs at that long table. The walls were all paneled in a beautiful wood finish, and at the head of the table was my great-grandfather, Grandpa Giles. He had been a bookkeeper, teacher and musician in the early 1900's. I remember him well as a little girl. Well, Grandpa stood up when I walked into the room and said, "Hello Janie, what can we do for you?" I looked around the room, and although I was not acquainted with most of the people, they were all smiling at me, and I was very comfortable. I replied, "Grandpa, I can't find my mistake in the books." He smiled and said, "8th column, 5th line." Although I felt like I didn't want to leave,

I closed the door. But in the morning, I quickly checked, and there was the mistake, as big as life in the 8th column, 5th line.

So I knew I had a council, and after reading, "Think and Grow Rich," in my 20's, I created the council of people I wanted to advise me. That council has grown and changed according to what I need, and right now it contains:

Jesus [compassion]
Albert Schweitzer [reverence for life]
My grandpa [joy]
Abe Lincoln [humor]
Viktor Frankl [observer]
Joe Campbell [storyteller]
My dad [nature]
Gandhi [persistence]
Florence Nightingale [power of words]
Leo Buscaglia [love]
Mother Theresa [toughness]
Leonardo Da Vinci [the ideas man]
Martin Luther [bravery]

It is a good idea to be at home with your council and ask for advice, and here is an example why it is so important: Life is all about decisions. Most of them are not life-changing, but sometimes when you look back on your path, you understand there are times that those tiny choices changed your life.

Thank You Mr. Frankl

My room was full of people talking and laughing, and I had a wonderful feeling of support. I could feel the energy of love caressing my skin, even though nobody was touching me. I had been experiencing something called somatoparaphrenia, which means feeling that you don't have ownership of one of your limbs.

My right hand and I were no longer on a first name basis. I had renamed her, "THE CLAW." Imagine that a part of your body had a mind of its own, and you could no longer trust it. You may have the thought of carrying a glass of water to the table when your rebellious hand throws the glass across the room. The claw may grab a person you are in conversation with in an inappropriate part of their body. Your arm could burst into a bout of fiery pain, or you could not even be aware that you closed your hand in the car door or picked a hot pan off the stove.

On this day, I was exercising the claw with a stress ball. I didn't understand many of the words being said, but I was totally loving the feeling of being loved. Suddenly the Claw took command, and she smashed the ball against my head hard enough to break it open. Green goo ran down my long hair and over my face. The room became silent, and time seemed to stop. It was like watching a cartoon where the Roadrunner is suspended over the cliff, and everything stops ... waiting ... you are aware of his thoughts, but everyone else is frozen, until he decides what to do next.

The strange thing about a stroke is that although I had trouble understanding what people were saying, and an even harder problem expressing myself, there were so many things I still remembered. My council was still there, and at this time Dr. Viktor Frankl came to me and said, "There is nothing you can do about the stoke, but you have the power to react to this situation anyway you want."

Dr. Frankl was a Jewish Psychiatrist during W.W.II; he had been in 5 different camps. He was used as a test guinea pig, starved, humiliated, and made to live through things we can't even imagine.

He was a master of resilience. His book, "Man's Search for Meaning," tells us that everything can be taken from us except our attitude. He saw people that went to the gas chambers weeping and fighting, and people that went praying to their God, singing his praises. Both types of people went to the gas chamber, but they went with different attitudes. I couldn't do anything today about my situation, but my attitude was mine.

The dragon called "Stoke" tries to steal a person's dignity. I could cry because my head really hurt, and I was very embarrassed, and all these people that loved me would spread a soothing balm of sympathy, or I could face this dragon and laugh, and if he thought he could defeat me, he better think again. Well, at least he wouldn't defeat me without a fight. I chose to laugh. I chose to take the one thing, the only thing in my power, that was my attitude, and laugh. And that tiny choice changed my life. At that moment, I was choosing to heal. Nobody else in the room knew the importance of that moment except me. Nobody saw the dragon or heard Dr. Frankl, but it was a beginning for me, and win or lose, I was in the game.

Treatments

Dr. Levine, the amazing neurologist, came to see me. Jim asked, wasn't there a surgery he could do - anything? Jim is a very scientifically trained man, and he believes in science and medicine. Dr. Levine answered that the arteries in my head were so twisted there was nothing he could do. I looked into his eyes and asked very slowly, "I die?" The doctor, who quite obviously received an "A" in bedside manner, took my hand and said, "I don't know, nobody knows when any of us will die. You have a very rare disease, and every day you are alive your odds go up."

When Jim asked what we did next, he said there was nothing to do. He told us that the vessels were so malformed that there was no treatment; I would be given a blood thinner, until the clots in my head were dissolved. Then he looked at me and said very gently, "I will support anything you choose to do."

Really, we live in the United States ... there is a drug for everything. Just watch T.V. and you will see a drug for every condition. How could I have something that they couldn't poison or cut out? Looking back, I wonder why I wasn't frightened. I would like to think it was because I had a strong faith, but I think I had grabbed onto Dr. Levine's words as a promise. Here was a very learned neurosurgeon who didn't know if I was going to die right now. There was hope, or at least a place to start. Hope is a super-charge to that fighting spirit inside.

Gifts in Many Forms

I was blessed everyday with people making the trip to the hospital in Madison.

My sisters and brothers came, even though it was a long trip and they had busy lives, with kids and jobs and all the extras life sends us. They showered me with loving support. Other people came too, friends and people I was surprised to see. They brought me wonderful gifts. Many of them were homemade and all of them filled with a loving spirit. They tried to wake my senses, they brought favorite foods trying to tempt my taste buds to wake up, and essential oils to stir my memory. A potter brought a specially-designed vase, and people brought chocolates, lots and lots of chocolates and flowers. An old roommate brought a beautiful book of paintings of ancient mythological goddesses. She told me not to forget I was a goddess too. That was the last thing I felt like, but by now nobody really expected me to talk, so I nodded smiled and said, "Thank you." But it was one visitor that helped me to see a truth. The lady was only an acquaintance, and she was visiting her husband in the hospital. She told me that he was having a real hard time, and she wished he had a better attitude. She smiled and said, "I sure wish you could talk to him, because he sure is not making friends with the nursing staff." She didn't stay long, but her words did stay with me. For the first time since the stroke I wondered, "Who was I going to be now? What would my purpose be?"

I wondered, "What could I do for this man?" I knew him to always have a smile and he was a good guy. He needed my help. What could have happened? I felt like my deepest, darkest fear had descended on me. When I would see someone that couldn't speak their thoughts, I could see in their eyes all those thoughts moving around in their head wishing to be expressed, and I felt a sadness, wondering what wisdom we were missing, and I wanted to run away. Perhaps I didn't run fast enough, because that demon had captured me and dammed up my words, and stolen what I thought would be my life's work.

"Well Sky, what would you do about this situation we are in?" I imagined she would say, "Not lay here and whine! Do something." I got up and grabbed my IV pole and went for a walk. Slowly I walked past the nurses' station and smiled. They asked, "Where are you off to?" I smiled back and said, "Walk." At the elevator, I pushed the up button and remembered the floor he was on; I was feeling pretty proud of myself. I found the room my friend was in and listened as he told me about the pain he was in and that nobody would answer his button, and that they said they were waiting for more tests. I patted his hand, shook my head, "No" and said, "Worry" - the closest I could get to, "Don't worry."

Then I went to the nurses' station, pointed to myself, and said, "Nurse"- then to my friend's room and said, "Shock." Both nurses jumped to their feet and ran to his room. I, on the other hand, headed to the elevator and my room. I got back in bed and thought perhaps there was still a place for me. I was asleep before I decided what that place was.

Going Home

I wanted to go home! The doctors did not want me to go home, which I did not understand. If there was nothing they could do, I needed to get to work on a plan. Finally, Dr. Muhammed Khasru, who spent time with me every day and appeared to be able to read minds of the people whose words were stuck in a log jam, said in frustration, "When you can do your addition tables up to 7, you can go home." I am betting he had a first-grader at home, and addition was a big issue in his life. Well now it was a big issue in my life too. I asked for some paper and started working. The next day when he came in, I handed him my addition tables. I did not tell him that a cleaning lady had shown me how to create these masterpieces that looked like a four-year-old had drawn them. He looked at me and said, "Okay, go home - tomorrow."

That night, a male nurse with a ponytail down his back came in to check on me. He asked if there was anything they could do for me this last night before I went home. I surprised him when I answered, "Chakras balanced." After a minute he said, "How about a massage?" The massage felt good, and I knew massage could become a piece of my healing.

Michelangelo said, "To touch is to give life." It seems as if science is proving this to be true. We know that touch activates the brain's orbitofrontal cortex and releases the hormone oxytocin. We feel less threatened, and we also feel a sense of connection. There have been studies involving neonatal units to nursing homes, and every group of people seems to be healthier when they are touched. It is helpful when you rub your own skin, because whenever we are touched, activity along the vagus nerve is increased. The vagus nerve runs from the abdomen to the brainstem, and when stimulated, it releases serotonin, the feel-good hormone. It also reduces blood pressure and anxiety.

It has been proven that petting a dog or a cat can release the serotonin, because touching and being touched have the same benefits.

Since I was right across from the nurses' station when the nurse went back to it, I heard someone ask what I had needed, and he answered that I wanted my chakras balanced. They laughed, and I heard someone say that they thought it more likely that it would be my checkbook I wanted balanced, because I was doing numbers all day.

Discharge

Becca was my designated driver for the trip home. The doctors came in with the latest instructions:

1. Since the stroke happened near my inner ear, I would most surely experience something called motion sickness, when I moved my head too quickly or when I rode in a vehicle. Well, at least I was familiar with this symptom. I probably experienced motion sickness as I traveled down the birth canal, and it had not lessened over the next 46 years. Motion sickness I could deal with.
2. I could not lift anything over 2 pounds. If I lifted something as heavy as a gallon of milk, one or more of my arteries may collapse and very likely cause death.

3. I was not to strain when I made a bowel movement for that same reason. I wondered, "Do people try to strain?"
4. They would contact a speech therapist at the Portage hospital, and I would go there for therapy.
5. I would need to have my blood tested because of the high level of blood thinners.
6. They told me to remember that every day I was alive raised the odds for me, but to think about getting my affairs in order, because the arteries were not expected to open.

Dr. Khasru pushed the wheelchair downstairs, and then he gave me his personal cell phone number and told me I could call day or night if I had any problem. He asked my permission to use my case in a paper he was presenting.

I was on my way home, and all seemed good. I was so tired when we got home, I was happy to get as far as the couch. The steps to my bedroom seemed like a mountain right now. I laid there and listened to Jim and the girls, as they told me stories about work and fun, until suddenly it was harder and harder to breathe. The cold fingers of fear were grabbing my heart. I was sure it was all starting again, and I was 90 minutes from the hospital. I didn't want to die here in front of all of them.

As calmly as possible I said, "I don't feel well; I can't breathe," and handed them the number to call Dr. Khasru. The fear was making it harder and harder to breathe. He answered and asked to talk to me. Immediately, he asked me to put the phone on my chest and then just to breath into the phone. After a minute he said, "You are not having a stroke. You are having an asthma attack. I said, "Don't have asthma." He asked if there were a lot of flowers in the room. I looked around and had to laugh. I doubted there was a flower anywhere within 10 miles, except in the room with me, including a cart-full that we brought from the hospital. "Jane drink some coffee, and get the flowers out of your house! Call back in a half hour if it isn't much better." He repeated, "In **30 minutes** get back to the hospital, if it isn't much better." Very slowly, I told him I can't drink coffee; I hate it. He laughed, "Good sentence, drink a coke, get some caffeine in."

This conversation set a strong imprint on me, and whenever I felt scared or heard my head pound, I drank a coke. It was a hard habit to break.

I looked at the people standing around the couch looking at me, and I felt expectation hanging in the air. Inside of me, I felt as if I had become a square peg in a round hole. For the last 24 years, I had set the intention that this home would be an oasis for the people that lived or visited here. Sometimes I felt like a juggler in the circus of life; I had poles of spinning plates, more and more plates all the time. Right now, many of those plates were wobbling, but the people around me, my family and friends, and the doctors, nurses and the cleaning lady were all catching those plates as they started to fall, and then starting them spinning again. Right now I was seeing double and couldn't make the images morph into one. I tried to say something, but the words wouldn't come out, and everyone else's words were not making sense, so all I could do was smile and close my eyes. I slid into the comfort and peace of sleep.

The days slipped into nights. The doctor had told me that every 24 hours I stayed alive, my chances were better. My very good friend and an old Pastor told me to trust the process, so I slept, and my body started to heal. My desire in telling this story is that caregivers need to understand that when a person has to work so hard to make a connection between thinking thoughts and speaking those thoughts, it often feels like the effort is too difficult, and it is easier to be quiet. I am telling this story for the person who has had something happen to their brain connection; just being quiet is not an option if you ever want to express yourself again. I know how difficult it is, and I am not 100% sure that if it happens again I will be able to fight as hard. It is a very hard fight, but I am 100% sure that I am happy I did fight. I also know if I can drag myself through the dismal swamp, so can you.

The Balance Sheet

As I laid there during the next few days I was home, I decided that if I was going to create a plan, I needed to take an inventory of what was going on in my life. If anyone asked me if I wanted the good news or bad news first, I have always been a bad-news-first girl. I like to get it over, and then slowly decide what to do as I savor the good news like a delicious dessert.

Liabilities:

- Agnosia - This is trouble recognizing objects, people, sounds or smells. I always knew the people I loved, however other people looked very much alike to me which meant I lost names and faces from the past. This is one of the things that I still deal with in part. I must really focus to remember names and faces. I had no sense of smell or taste. Those two senses travel together. Because of this, I was losing weight at record speed. In fact, after a week at home, I had an appointment at the neurology clinic for my weekly check.

  I told Dr. Levine that I thought I had cancer now. He smiled and asked, "Don't you think a stroke was life-changing enough?" Dr. Khasru smiled and asked, "How did you come to this diagnosis?" Well, I told them how much weight I had lost in three weeks, and that I was barely moving. They became serious and told me my body was doing so much work I couldn't imagine. It was trying to stay alive and needed as much energy as possible, so it was eating any fat I had stored. Plus, I needed to eat more. I have to admit, I was barely eating, because food gagged me. So many people brought me food that our refrigerator was packed. They made their favorites and mine. It didn't matter if it was hot or cold, Italian or Chinese, all food tasted like what I would imagine wallpaper paste would taste like. Meals became a great stress for me. Jim loves food and could eat under any circumstance. He believes, due to strong culinary teaching from his Italian grandmother, that food and wine are the answer to ANY ill health. So, mealtime became me pushing food around my plate and trying to gag down a few bites, with Jim watching me and pleading with me to try a few more bites. As far as sounds went, after a short time of listening to people, the words made no sense to me. I thought they may be speaking Martian, or what I think Martian would sound like.

- Amnesia - This is a period of time is that is forgotten. I lost a great deal of memories during the time my girls were growing up. This is a sadness, but in the last year or so, a memory will pop up and call out, "Look at me!" I know that it is really my memory and not borrowed from Jim or the girls. I have hope that more and more memories will free themselves from the tangles and trapped cells of my brain. They were given up for dead, but they perhaps were only comatose and will find their way to the surface.

- Anomia - This is a problem finding key words and word retrieval. Most people with brain attacks understand this frustration. We are not talking about an, "it is on the tip of my tongue" kind of thing, but it is a black wall with the word locked in a safe, and you don't have the combination. Pure Frustration!

- Aphasia - This is when words don't come out right. The strange thing is, you often see the word and are ready to say it, but between your tongue and your lips there is an exchange and the word that comes out is not what you were expecting. You are as surprised as everyone else. This is the time that many people give up trying to be a part of the conversation. The frustration of not being understood is difficult, but I think that the embarrassment is the worst part. I would tell the girls to cook my bird (cockatiel) rather than feed him. They would laugh and say, "It will be so little meat. Are you sure?" A perfect example of aphasia was when our daughter, Maria, was dating a young man named Ron. I had only met him a couple times before the stroke. One night we were standing in the kitchen and he said to me, "I was told you are a hypnotist, and I am a smoker. Do you have any luck with smokers?" In my head was the thought, "Me a hypnotist? That is a very funny joke." In my wildest dreams, I could not imagine having the control of my words and voice to help people with hypnosis. But I looked right at Ron and said, "Yes, I have my best sex with young fathers." My crazy daughters laughed wildly, and this poor young man just looked at me. I had wanted to say, "... my best success ..."! Ron showed great patience, and while my family would finish my sentences with the best intentions, he would sit and wait for me to gather my thoughts and then start the long process of pushing the words I meant out from my lips. Ron married Maria.

- Anosognosia - This is a denial that there is any disability. I may not be the Queen of Denial (that is my mother), but I am a high level princess. It is important to be aware of what is going on in your body, and it is important to not become afraid and suspect the worst possible condition. Here is the perfect example of the Queen's denial or perhaps it is very real manifesting with the idea of "fake it until you make it" - you decide: I was 10-years-old and running on ice. Yes, I had been told not to run on ice, but the freedom you feel when you slide as light as air, while the cold wind at your back is pushing you along, was irresistible. This feeling is intoxicating. On this day I fell face-first and knocked out my new front permanent teeth. Actually, they were hanging by a string. I got home, the queen had pushed them back into the socket and told me that for a week I would only eat or drink water and broth, and after a week I could graduate to Jell-O and ice cream shakes. Then she told me not to worry, that my teeth would solidify into the socket, if I followed the plan. I believe today that my mother had pulled this dental plan out of thin air, but when I was 10, she was an authority figure, and I was scared, thinking I was facing a toothless future. This was a perfect scenario for an imprint, and a new belief was formed. My teeth did solidify, and I still have them. I did know that there were many things wrong, but I also knew that it would not be helpful to focus on what was wrong. I needed to focus on what was right, and whenever I was able to do that, it made me feel better. When the need to focus is so strong, you have to remember that they put blinders on horses so they are not aware of the distractions all around them. I needed blinders to remember it didn't matter if I couldn't do something "yet;" it didn't matter if I said something foolish; it didn't even matter if I shocked people. I was focused on healing. I needed to fake it, until I could make it. In my little town, there were many people ready to help me, like the girls at the bank. Once I was back home, I would attempt to do the bank deposit for the business. Very carefully, I would hold a piece of cardboard across the numbers in a straight line, so as not to lose my place, but I seldom got the deposit right. They would say so kindly, "Almost all right this time, only a couple checks off!" Or, on the odd day that I was right they would say, "Great job, Jane; it is all right." I could choose to accept their kindness, or be embarrassed and not attempt the deposit. If you choose to be embarrassed, you give your power away; that is no way to heal. It was important not to give any power away, because I was on the edge of a cliff with my foot on a banana peel.

- Somatoparaphrenia - This is the denial of ownership of a limb. This was a bit backward for me. I completely knew my right arm was mine. I had named it "the claw." The problem was that the claw did not think it belonged to me. It was in total anarchy and followed no rules. If the hand/arm was not being held, it would grab a person in very inappropriate places on their person. It was known to grab glasses off faces, and that was one of its better tricks. One time, I was in my friend's house, and she was showing me some redecorating she was doing. I asked what she was planning on doing with the windows. She answered that she was using the curtains that were in my hands. I had walked past the table and grabbed the curtains without any knowledge that I had done that. This was why the thought of going to a store without a strait jacket on could send me into a panic attack.

I wondered if you would be sent to jail as a kleptomaniac if you had a thief for a hand. Has anyone used that as a defense? I would burn myself, because even though you don't have feelings in your fingers, it is still necessary to use a pot holder. I slammed the car door on my hand and was aware of it because of the lack of my range of motion and the look of horror on the driver's face, not because of any pain. Yet at times, I could be sitting on the couch watching TV and the nerve pain could take my breath away. My plan was to ignore as much as I could, and not tell anyone, because I thought of it as an entity and believed talking about it, or even thinking about it overly much, would give it power. Hypnosis helped me, because I could go upstairs and put myself into trance, and 15 minutes later I could be down stairs with a fully anesthetized arm. One more odd thing about this symptom was that I could not distinguish where my hand stopped and Jim's started, if he was holding my hand. For some reason, this was very disturbing. I felt as if I had no borders to my body. Over and over during the day, I would say to myself, "Better and better every day, in every way." I knew every cell in my body was listening to me.

- Diplopia - This is double vision, and when I was focusing and rested I could pull the two images together, but if I was not consciously focusing my eyes, I would see two of anything in front of me. It was an illusion, and I knew it was an illusion, but if I had been asked to point to what was real, I would have been unable to do that. Continually, I told myself, "This is an illusion; rest your eyes and then focus." After a bit of rest, the two images became one again. After a few months, I got prisms in my glasses.

- Horner's Syndrome - This has a couple of pieces to it. First, my left pupil was dilated, and sunlight was very painful; even a cloudy day was difficult for me without sunglasses. The most obvious symptom of Horner's is that if I was overheated, the blood vessels on the left side of my face would dilate under the skin to create flushing. I don't mean that I would blush, but that one side of my face would become bright red, and at the same time, the other side of my face would blanch, becoming the whitest of white. This makes me look as if I was wearing a mask. The line of demarcation is straight and definite. Bright red on one side, from the hairline to the chin, and the palest of white on the other half.

- Foot drop - You may have seen people that have had a stroke, and they walk with an exaggerated high step. The reason for this is that if you have foot drop, you can be walking along and the front of your foot drops, as if the muscles don't have the strength to hold your toes up. You are not aware of it, until you trip. In addition, I really had little depth perception as to where the floor was.

- Vertigo - This was the hardest symptom for me psychologically, and it remains difficult 17 years after the stroke. I don't experience it as much as I once did, but because of the damage to the area near my inner ear, it happens more than I like, and it never fails to scare me. The only real symptom of this, other than the blood pounding in my ears, which I had before the stroke, was being so very dizzy. But when it happens, whether it is because I have turned my head too fast, or whether it happens without a trigger - just because of a damaged area in my brain - I immediately go into fight or flight mode.

- Inability to see auras - I don't know what or if there is a name for this, but since I was a child I saw auras, or colored energy fields, around people. A person that sees auras learns quickly to rely on them to understand people more fully, and to occasionally walk away from someone. Although I continued to feel energy, I saw no colors. I remember the first time I walked into a large grocery store, I wanted to curl up under the produce counter. I felt like I was physically being hit by the amount of energy everywhere, but I couldn't decipher the positive and negative energies, because the colors were gone. Recently, a young autistic man talked to me, and I told him what it felt like to me when I was in a large crowd and asked him if he understood. He nodded, tears in his eyes, and walked away. I heard him say to his mother. "She is like me; she understands." The colors were a safety net for me, and when I needed them the most, they had disappeared. I saw a shimmering light around everything but I missed the colors. It was a weakness to use them to judge people, and perhaps that was my lesson. I am happy to say they are coming back.

- Panic attacks - These were now a monster that was always hiding around a corner, ready to jump out at me. They may have thought I was an easy mark, because as I was leaving the hospital, I was told that if I lifted anything heavier than a half-gallon of milk, or even strained when I went to the bathroom, I would risk the clots that had not dissolved breaking free, or the liners of my misshapen arteries letting go of their walls to suck together. I admit that those were pretty good reasons to panic, but it really doesn't matter. You see, whether you have a good reason to panic, or be angry or frustrated, or you don't, it doesn't matter. Your body must deal with the results. Our subconscious mind doesn't know if something is real or imagined, so it will react as if it was real. Expose a

34

fake as quickly as possible to do the least amount of damage. This is one of the best techniques I know to combat those fearsome, heart-pounding, breath-stealing monsters. Imagine a rectangle; you breathe in along the short side and exhale along the long side. For example, breathe in through your nose to the count of three and out through your mouth to the count of six. You can also try to breathe in to the count of four and exhale to eight. When we get frightened, we breathe very shallowly, and our lungs fill with carbon dioxide. Imagine as you breathe in, that fresh oxygen is filling your lungs and calming you as you breathe out the carbon dioxide. Another wonderful part of this is that during a panic attack, when you feel out of control, you can do this to regain control. You are in control of your breath, and for that moment, that is all you need. This is the time to remember what General George Patton said about bravery, "If bravery is a quality which knows not fear, I have never seen a brave man. All men are frightened. The more intelligent they are, the more they are frightened. The courageous man is the man who forces himself, in spite of his fear, to carry on." It makes me laugh when I hear someone say, "I would die if that happened." No, most things won't kill you, but we always have the choice to decide how we will live. Courage is really just doing the next best thing. Someone who has no fear is a bit psychotic; fear can be healthy, but it is your reaction to it that really matters. Move ahead with courage!

- Lack of energy - My energy was so low that I could have slept, sat up and gone back to sleep. I decided that I needed a purpose each day, and mine would be to feed my bird, Murray, and make the bed. My quilt was too heavy for me to lift, so Jim would move it in the morning and at night, and I could do the rest of the bed covers, and then nap on the couch until I could gather the energy to feed Murray. Even if you are not a person who asks for help, you will be now. Rebecca and Amanda were both living away. Maria announced that she was taking a semester off to help me. I fought with her, but it was a weak fight, because we all knew I needed help. Maria helped me until Gina was home from high school, then Gina and Jim picked up the rest of my care, so Maria could go and help Ron with his new business. I am so grateful for her decision.

- Stuttering - If I felt rushed or uneasy, I stuttered continually. It was not just speaking words that made me stutter. I stuttered when I wrote anything. I felt as if I was holding my finger on the key of an electric typewriter too long. I would write my name as "Jaannnee Govooooooni." Even if I didn't stutter write, I still had a great deal of frustration with my writing. Here is an example of my writing from therapy:

- Hearing loss - Lastly, I had lost a great deal of my hearing.

Okay that was my rather long list of liabilities but I also had assets.

Assets

- My organs were in great working order, with the exception of my brain, ears and eyes.

- I had not lost my balance, which seemed to surprise everyone. I had taken my first yoga class twenty years before my stroke. My balance was not great for the "old me," but still better than average. The balance sheet appeared to be very unbalanced, and if this was a financial page, I definitely would be in the red, but it wasn't a financial statement; it was a card game, and I was holding a full house. I had love ... and there is nothing more powerful.

Chapter 3

CHAKRAS

Many medical, mental health, energy, acupuncture, and yoga practitioners work with the basic seven energy centers, called chakras. They are found from the base of our spine to the crown of our head. Think of them as little spinning disks of energy, each affecting an area of our body physically and emotionally. The reason I wanted my chakras balanced was that a few months before my stroke, Becca was living in Milwaukee when she needed emergency intestinal surgery. My friend, Shari, came to see Becca right after she returned from surgery and balanced her chakras, telling me that she would have no trouble with her recovery. It was amazing! The nurses came in to get Becca up for the first time, and she had no trouble at all. The nurses were amazed at the ease in which she was moving, and they were more amazed the next day when she was supposed to try and walk in the hall, and she walked more than twice the distance they expected her to be able to move.

At first I thought perhaps it was a placebo effect or a self-fulfilling prophecy. Maybe she believed my friend, and it changed her belief. All that may have happened, except Becca was asleep. Shari worked silently, and when she spoke, it was to me, out of Becca's hearing. She came back later and talked to Becca, but Becca had already been the Star Patient. That is why I wanted my chakras balanced. Here is a bit of information about the chakras:

The **Root Chakra, 1st,** is found at the base of the spine, and it is thought of as the color red. It deals psychologically with feeling safe. Physically, this root chakra deals with your immune system and your legs and bones. It really has to do with your health and all the things found in your physical world. Emotionally, the way you know you are not balanced is when you find yourself fearful about life. Listen to your words. Are you talking about what scares you about life? If you are balanced, you are healthy and feel good about life and your future, and you find it easy to live in the moment. Too much of root energy makes you feel heavy, sluggish, and bored. You may also be so materialistic that you become a hoarder, a workaholic and a Scrooge! Too little, and you deal with anxiety and fear big time. Maybe you feel spacey or restless. You may resist any structure, and feel trapped if you think about rules, and you have little self-discipline. So, what can you do about balancing the root chakra on your own? First eat proteins, nuts, beans and root vegetables. You need to move your body; this has been indicated by the latest scientific research. Exercise beats Prozac in study after study. The ancient wisdom that deals with these energy centers says you should play more, walk more, do more gardening and get more sleep. If you want to heal the root chakra, work with your hands. Visualize that little red spinning disk spinning to the right, unless you have too much energy and are finding life a little monotonous, then spin to the left. If you are musical, you can chant or tone the sound, "ol," the same sound as you hear in the word, "pole." Breathe a complete breath, because when we become anxious, we tend to breathe very shallowly and don't exhale completely. When you consciously think about breathing, take a good breath through your nose and exhale through your mouth. If I feel my root chakra is out of balance, and I find myself falling for all the fear tactics of the news, I may put on my garnet ring or put a piece of hematite in my pocket. I don't think rocks are like magic beans, but like everything else in life, they have their own energy, and for me rocks remind me to breathe and they remind me what my intention is for that day. I like to utilize the crystal rock that people who can feel rock energy say works best in my situation. Essential oils also affect our bodies and emotions, so I may sniff or wear an oil that is known for a certain situation I am experiencing. The root chakra seems to be nurtured by cedar wood, clove, pepper, patchouli and vetiver.

The **Sacral Chakra, 2nd,** is orange and is found in the lower back and pelvic area. It is physically in charge of the stomach and sex organs. The root chakra was more physical, and this one is emotional. The second energy center is about feelings, so people who have a balanced sacral chakra have healthy boundaries, and they nurture everyone and themselves. They can feel pain and pleasure. The challenge here is guilt. And if they have too much of this energy, they may be emotionally unstable, too sensitive, obsessive, or may have sexual or sensual addictions. Not enough Sacral energy, and they could be emotionally numb, fear change, pleasure and pain. This is also the energy center that deals with sexual problems in both men and woman. Your toning sound would be, "oo," like the word, "two." This center deals with water. The human body is 60% water, and this chakra deals with water. So if you are healing this very creative part of your body, drink water or juice. I don't mean the sugary juice either; we are not hummingbirds! I am talking about the ones you make in your juicer. The activities to balance this chakra are, of course, to visualize the orange center spinning right if you are in the deficient place, and left if you have too much sacral energy. It is also helpful to be in water, and it doesn't matter if you are bathing in your tub or swimming in the ocean. If you are swimming in the ocean, it matters a little because it is also about enjoying senses, and you can't feel sand, hopefully, in your tub, or smell salty wind on your face. Carry a moonstone or an opal. The oils to use are sandalwood, ylang ylang, jasmine, cinnamon, or tangerine. You want to become more flexible, so you could do yoga or dance. Dancing is a wonderful sensual experience, and you don't have to go anywhere or buy anything. Remember the Mark Twain quote, "Sing like nobody's listening, love like you've never been hurt, dance like nobody's watching, and live like it's heaven on earth."

The **3rd** chakra is the **Solar Plexus Chakra** and is found above the abdomen on our body. It is the color yellow, and the organs that it is associated with it are the pancreas and the adrenal glands. This one is all about ego, and when our ego is balanced, we are self-confident, disciplined and have good self-esteem. Shame is the challenge of this energy center, and if you have too much of this energy, you blame everyone else and are overly competitive and perhaps domineering. If your ego needs to be strengthened, then you may show signs of poor self-esteem, lack energy, and be fearful and submissive. If you feel your 3rd chakra needs to be balanced, start by eating some grains and complex carbs, and get moving! This chakra is about releasing things you are attached to, and not just things but anger, shame, blame, guilt, and fear too. It is about nurturing yourself and laughing. You can carry a citrine or tiger's eye stone, and chant the tone "aw" as in awesome. The oils for the solar plexus are lemon, ginger, peppermint, bergamot, lavender, and rosemary.

The 4th energy center is the **Heart**. The color is green, and that is a healing color. Physically, the 4th chakra is about the heart, lungs, arms and thymus. As you would expect, this is all about loving and feeling loved. If you are balanced, you love yourself and are compassionate to others. People with balanced heart chakras are non-judgmental and peaceful. If you have too much heart energy, you may be codependent, a martyr, jealous or just a people pleaser. Too little makes you antisocial, withdrawn, critical, lonely and intolerant. To balance your heart energy, it would be good for you to eat vegetables, especially dark green, leafy vegetables. The rock that helps balance this chakra is rose quartz, and your tone for this chakra is "A" like the sound of "play." Some oils for the heart chakra are marjoram, rose, yarrow, bergamot, and lemongrass. This chakra is all about acceptance, forgiveness, gratitude, and love of yourself and others.

The **Throat Chakra** is 5th and is in charge of the throat, mouth, ears, hands and thyroid. The color is blue. This one is all about self-expression and creating, and if you are balanced, you communicate clearly and truthfully. People with balanced throat chakras are also good listeners and express themselves creatively. Too much energy here makes people talk excessively; they are poor listeners, gossip, and they are loud and can't keep secrets. If you don't have enough throat energy, you may be excessively shy and have a weak voice. The thought of speaking in front of people throws you into great fear. To balance this chakra, you want to eat raw fruit. Music is a balancer of this chakra; sing, chant, create music, or listen to songs that make your heart fill with joy. If you are chanting a tone it will be, "ee" like in "speak," and you may want to carry or wear turquoise or sapphire stones and use eucalyptus, frankincense, or sage oil.

The **Third Eye Chakra, 6th,** is between the eyebrows, and deals with the pineal and pituitary glands. The color is indigo. With this chakra, we are called to witness ourselves as we really are. A balanced person with a good third eye chakra is wise. They are going to have good intuition, so they know that they can trust their gut. They also possess a good memory; in fact, they will even remember their dreams. These are people who can see the big picture, and they want everyone's life to be better. If you have too much of this purple energy, you may have trouble concentrating, have nightmares, or perhaps become delusional. Too much and you may fantasize, and too little you don't have much, if any, imagination. If you are deficient in third eye energy, your thinking may be inflexible, and you may find yourself in denial and have a poor memory. Here are some ideas about balancing this chakra: Create visual beauty; if you created a beautiful garden, you could nurture both your first and 6th chakras. The bottom five chakras deal with your life in your body, but the 6th and 7th deal with your higher consciousness, so there is not a food that will balance these two chakras. In fact, abstaining from food is better for balancing them. The stones for the third eye chakra are amethysts and purple fluorites. If you want to use an oil to balance the third eye chakra, use lavender, pine, sage, jasmine, or peppermint. Possibly the best thing you can do to nurture this chakra is to slow down and make time to meditate, where you might tune or chant "om," like the word, "home," and look at all the beauty around you, breathe, and drink a glass of water.

The **Crown Chakra, 7th**, is found at the top of the head and physically deals with the head, cerebral cortex, upper spine and hair. Psychologically, it is all about the Spirit and our connection to God, whoever you imagine that to be. It is about remembering that you are the beloved child of God, a child of the Universe, and a part of this web that we all belong to. The color associated with this chakra is violet or white. If you find yourself balanced, you are a wise master. You have an open mind that is filled with compassion, love, harmony and peace. Too much crown chakra energy could create a religious addiction, where you are not connected to others and are dissociated from your body. Too little of crown energy, and you may find yourself materialistic, spiritually uncertain, and mentally inflexible. To balance this chakra, pray, meditate, learn, and create. Breath and pure water are important for this chakra. The oils to use are lotus, rose, frankincense, sandalwood, myrrh, and spruce; and the stones to use are diamonds, clear quartz, or Herkimer diamonds.

Yoga

Yoga would be a big piece in my healing plan, not because I thought yoga was the best way to heal, but because it is a way to heal more than just our body. Yoga is a philosophy and a set of practices. Some of the oldest pottery found along the Nile, Euphrates and the Indus Rivers have pictures of yoga poses on them. Yoga can make our muscles flexible, our joints feel free, and give our bodies a sense of balance. The philosophy of yoga is about wholeness. Our body and mind are not separate, and we need not be separate from the Great One either. Everything is in a constant state of change. Yoga means "to join," and the thought is that we are fragmented, so when we move in yoga, we are moving the physical, intellectual, emotional, and spiritual aspects of who we are into alignment. When we are in alignment, we have vitality.

We are all joined and alike in many ways. We are human, but then we divide ourselves by what we have learned to think we are. In hypnosis, I think of it as imprints, and I ask people to write down who they are - every characteristic they can use to name themselves - and then I ask where each idea came from. We come into the world a blank canvas, and people tell us who we are, and we start to believe that. We too often become who people say we are. "You have a temper just like..." or, "you never could focus and sit quietly..." and on and on. Then we live to the expectation we have been given. The philosophy of yoga believes that energy has five patterns, and although we all contain all five patterns, one of the patterns vibrates as our primary energy. Everything is a possibility. If you have ever studied palmistry, your hand shape shows uniqueness. The patterns are:

1. Earth energy, which is solid and stable. People with this energy are more conventional, and their creativity is more practical and connected to nature.
2. Fire energy is outgoing, vital and enthusiastic. People who have this energy are never still for long; they need to move. They are fond of being outdoors, and they are the leaders.
3. Air energy is mental and people with this energy are good communicators. These people would be good with all of the technology of today's life. They are in control of their emotions.

4. People with water energy are attracted to the arts. They are very sensitive and have some trouble keeping their feet firmly on the ground.

5. People have elements of all of the above types of energy. The 5th element is wind or space, and here is where we can see science and ancient wisdom cross paths. Everything, including people, have this type of energy. The ancients say wind energy carries the possibilities and potentials of the human existence. Science says that there are both waves and particles. We are also waves and particles, changing all the time.

To restore balance to the body, think of these energies moving through every asana (yoga position), and listen to your body, and ask what it needs from you. I knew that my body couldn't do any inversions. It felt as if my head was hanging on for dear life, but that meant I needed as flexible and strong of a spine as I could create.

Yoga should never hurt; you feel the stretch, but stop before pain. You don't use willpower to force yourself to go deeper into a pose, but surrender your will into the poses using your breath.

I could do twists sitting in a chair. I could stand in mountain pose and use a chair to move into tree pose. I could still do cat and cow poses and sit in butterfly pose. For now, it was enough for me to remember that everything changes. If we are to heal, we must feel that we have some power over our life. Yoga gives me that feeling. It was the way I learned to deal with stress in my twenties, and would be a piece in my healing now. I had the power to change, to align my body, mind and spirit and to heal.

Here are a few of the benefits of yoga:

- Blood pressure, pulse and respiratory rates decreases
- EEG alpha, theta, delta and beta waves increase during yoga meditation
- Cardiovascular efficiency increases
- Gastrointestinal function normalizes
- Flexibility and joint range of motion increases
- Endocrine function normalizes
- Grip strength increases
- Hand-eye coordination improves
- Dexterity skills and reaction time increase
- Posture improves
- Strength and resilience increases
- Energy and endurance levels increase
- Pain decreases
- Weight and sleep improves
- Immune system increases
- Balance and depth perception improves
- Feelings of well-being and a positive mood increase
- Anxiety and depression decrease
- Anger decreases

There was no doubt I needed Yoga!

If you don't know the power of yoga, there is not a more powerful story or testimonial for the power of this ancient practice than the story of Arthur Boorman. Arthur was a paratrooper in the Gulf War. When he came home hurt, he was told that he would never walk unassisted again. He believed the doctors, and they showed him on x-rays and tests that they were right. He sat for 15 years with his disability, until he saw an ad about yoga. He was 47 years-old and weighed 297 pounds, but something about the ad inspired him, and he started a program. In 10 months, he lost 140 pounds and was walking on his own. You can watch the transformation on YouTube, because his son documented his progress.

Qigong

Yoga is not the only healing art, of course. In the last five years, I have learned about Qigong. I learned about Spring Forest Qigong from my friend, Karyn, who is a master of Qigong and a follower of Master Chunyi Lin. If you were to watch people doing Qigong and Tai Chi, you would think they were very similar, but Tai Chi is actually a martial art, and Qigong is a healing art.

It is like yoga in that it creates greater flexibility and strength, reduces stress, and balances your energy. And like Yoga, Qigong has no religious attachment. The only connection I think they have to a faith system, is they believe and practice love, peace, and forgiveness. That is the center post for all faiths.

They do recharge your body's natural ability to heal. Qigong does not treat symptoms, but works to remove energy blocks. Then when the energy is balanced and flowing, health follows.

Here are a few things that can cause blockages: unbalanced emotions, poor nutrition, environment, the wrong medication, an injury, and even the weather and the change from season to season. By environment, I mean the people you have around you, along with the air you breathe. Environment can also include the way energy moves through your home. Feng Shui is a practice where you use the placement of your things in your house to create a healing environment.

It is understandable that symptoms are not the disease or the cause of the disease. Think about all the diseases that have the same symptoms; most diseases indicate a feeling of fatigue, and many have symptoms of headaches or sleeplessness. Most disease starts with our thoughts, and manifests in our body. Qigong is a beautiful, slow movement of energy that, had I learned about it earlier, would have been an important piece of my healing program. Now I use it daily, if only for a few minutes to stay healthy.

Energy

One of the things I love about energy healing is intention. Intention means to intend or plan something, or bring about a state. When you do energy healing, you call on the Master that you have the greatest respect for; for me this is Jesus. This is why I would walk with my hands on my head asking Jesus to send healing energy down through my hands into the crown of my head. I would imagine that healing light caressing my brain, and waking the cells up as it reconnected the neuro pathways.

My intention was to heal my brain, so my body could heal. I set this intention on my daily walk, but this was not the only time I set it. We need to remind ourselves over and over what we intend. Everything is easier when we do this, because all of us have things we must do that are not fun. If my intention is to have a clean house, that includes cleaning toilets. Cleaning toilets is not in the fun category, but if a clean house gives me enough pleasure, then even cleaning toilets is okay.

Perhaps you don't like to exercise, but you want a healthy body. If you want a healthy body enough, you find a way to move your body. Think out-of-the-box; what did you like as a child? For me my favorite exercise is hula hooping. Did you like to jump rope as a child? Or maybe you liked to ride your bike or walk. You don't need expensive machines or a gym membership, there is no excuse; just move your body.

When you wake up in the morning, set your intention for the day. Perhaps at noon, set it again, and when you go to bed, set the intention for a good night's sleep. This will keep your thought more focused on what you really want. Think of your thoughts and intentions like a radio station. There are thousands of radio waves circling us, but we tune into what we desire. I often want to listen to a country station, so my radio is preset to what I like, but if I travel out of range, or if there is a storm, I need to adjust the signal. Intention keeps your thoughts tuned to what you desire.

I saw a sign that said, "Don't tell your God about how big the storms are in your life, tell the storms about how big the God is in your life." Well, I had a big God. I had enough faith that I believed with every cell in my body that I could be healed, **if** it was part of the plan for my life. I could be healed as quickly as the Divine Breath decided to breathe into my face. I also knew I would be fine if that was not part of the divine plan. As of this moment, neither I, nor the best doctors around, knew what the plan was. I had made my wishes known, I wanted two more years until Gina graduated. It seemed to me God and I had an agreement; I would be the best mother I could be, and I would have the opportunity to get them all through high school. I believe most parents breathe a sigh of relief on that day. But if that was not to happen, there was a reason. But at the moment, the idea that I was to be healed was not clear to me, and because I was not privy to His plan, I would do everything I knew how to do to get healthy and carry out my plan.

I had love. Even though I felt like a tightrope walker, I had a support system that was like a tight safety net. There was Jim, strong and sure, never for even one minute did I doubt that he loved me and would stay no matter what happened. Becca was soft and nurturing and always seeing me as the person I had always been. Maria was more practical and helped with whatever needed to be done. Amanda pushed doors open, encouraging me to try a bit harder to find my way home, and Gina was my constant. She was the one that saved me the night of the stroke, and she was the reason I was fighting so hard. I needed two more years to finish my job.

That was only the beginning of my safety net. My mother drove me to therapy and told me normal family news. My sisters, brothers and sister-in law and brothers-in-law, even though they had busy lives, called, visited, and brought me things that would maybe tempt me to eat. I knew I could call any of them and they would do anything I asked. I had aunts and uncles, cousins and friends everywhere. I was a very, very blessed lady. At one time, I counted people in seven states and three countries that were praying for me. I had lived in the same small town for 22 years, and I have found that the people in small towns are wonderful, especially if you have a problem. You see, love trumps anything in a liability column.

THE HERO'S JOURNEY

On August 13th 1998, I started what the great mythologist Joseph Campbell, one of my council members, would call "the hero's journey." We are each the hero of our own story and will be forced onto the journey's path throughout our life. These journeys happen when a great change comes to us. It can be an illness, as it was for me, or a divorce, job loss, death of a loved one; there are too many changes and challenges to name. We must travel alone on what Campbell calls "the road of trials," but people along the road will help us learn lessons and encourage and comfort us. All the lessons will not be sweet and gentle lessons. Dragons are teachers along with wizards and angels. It is my experience that dragons travel in packs. It will be to your advantage to trust the very wise advice of David Lee, the stress management speaker, who tells us it is to our advantage to believe in reverse paranoia, or that everyone is there to help you, as everyone has a valuable gift for you. Yes, even the dragons.

The hero's journey is like the stories we all know like, "The Wizard of Oz," "The Lord of the Rings," "Narnia," "Harry Potter," or "Star Wars." We travel our own yellow brick road and find helpers like the lion, the tin man and the scarecrow. We get trapped in the dismal swamp for a time, and these helpers, no matter how wonderful they are, can only be that - helpers. We need to defeat our dragons with courage, love, strength, faith, humor, kindness, imagination and a grateful heart. When we have defeated our dragons, then Joseph Campbell says it is our job to return and share our story with those that come after us.

I am not sure we choose transformation. Perhaps we are all a bit like Frodo in "The Lord of the Rings," when he said to Gandalf, "I wish the ring would never have come to me. I wish that none of this would have happened." Gandalf answered, "So do all that live to see such times. But that is not for them to decide. All we have to decide is what to do with the time that is given us."

White Crows

My job is to listen to people, and sometimes hear things that they don't even hear themselves saying, and then help them make a plan to create the dream they long for. I am not talking about getting "stuff," I am talking about helping people access the best part of who they already are inside. When I think about what I have done as a career for the last 35 years, it is only to listen and then choose the right key to hand them. It is then their job to start unlocking the chains that hold them back. I am only the cheerleader, but I believe without a doubt in my mind, that we are each powerful beyond our imagination. It was said in Psalm 139:13 that we are "wonderfully made." Each of us is such a miracle.

We may have often been told that we can't do this or that, because that is the reality of society. Whenever you hear that you can't do something, create a list of the people that have proven that statement false. Think of the sailors that were told that the earth was flat and how that was reality until some sailors proved it false. Many people could not imagine someone walking on the moon, until Neil Armstrong did it. Most of us believe what people in authority tell us to believe, and that is natural; even animals give up after a short time. A jar of fleas will jump out of a jar, until you put a top on that jar. After they bump their little flea heads a few times, you can take the top off, and they won't jump out of the jar. An adult elephant needs a small rope to hold her, but a young elephant needs a chain. This is because that young elephant can't believe that it can't be free, and the old elephant can't believe that it can.

There is something known as a 'White Crow,' that is someone who is told they can't do something, like recover from hyper-fibro-dysplasia; and they believe it is possible and do heal. You see a crow is normally a black bird, and people often say all crows are black. If you find that one white crow, then you are unable to believe all crows are black, or that all people will die from something like hyper-fibro-dysplasia. 'White Crow' means hope. Here are a couple of other 'White Crows:"

In 1954, Roger Banister started to question the belief that if a human ran faster than a four-minute mile his heart would burst. He thought it just might be a false belief, and he might make it possible, so he put a little note in his shoe that said, "3:59 minutes," and he practiced running, always visualizing that 3:59-minute time. On May 28th, he broke the 4-minute mile with a time of 3:59:4 minutes. His record only lasted 46 days. It was no longer impossible.

What would happen if we all questioned what was possible? Would we break our own chains and find out they were only a small rope with just the illusion of chains? Would we be like Erik Weihenmayer, a blind man, who climbed the highest peaks in all seven continents?

In March of 1981, Morris Goodman crashed his plane and crushed his spinal cord, breaking his neck. He was fully paralyzed. He couldn't breathe, talk, or swallow. His only function left was that he could blink his eyes. His sister made a chart with pictures and words, and he would blink his communication. He blinked that he would walk out of the hospital by Christmas. The medical world said he couldn't live. Morris has said, "it didn't matter what they believed, it only mattered what I believed." He walked out of the hospital eight months later. Two years later, he spoke in sentences, and five years later, he walked freely.

Can we believe that one small man in India could bring down the largest empire of the 19th century without firing a shot? How far could we reach if we collected the stories of people who had done the impossible and when we were told that we couldn't do something, we smiled and worked to prove that we could do what we focused on, just like the amazing people that we modeled.

Medicine Wheel

If I was going to treat myself like a client, I would start as I always do, with the Medicine Wheel. Medicine wheels has intrigued me since I first learned about them. There is an ancient Hopi prophecy that is shared by many native people. The story goes that at the beginning of the world, the creator created the four races in four colors and gave each of them a job to do, and if they each did their part, the world's people would live in one sacred circle. This is how the jobs were handed out: the red race was to take care of the earth. They were given the secrets of the plants, herbs and food. The yellow race was given the knowledge of the air. They had the secrets of breath and the spiritual world. The black race had the secrets of water - the most powerful of the elements. They were given the deepest knowledge of the human emotions. The white race was given the knowledge of fire. Fire creates, consumes, and moves life. The prophecy says when all the nations get together, they will all live in peace.

It doesn't matter if you find a wheel in Tibet, Africa, North or South America, or in one of the Celtic countries, it will be divided in those four colors, red, white, black and yellow. They have been found all over the world. They show the four directions, four elements and the four areas of health - mind, body, spirit and emotions.

If healing is holistic or integrative, it uses Eastern and Western medicine. Over and over I hear doctors or nurses say, "I use scientifically proven medicine," and they make unkind comments and dismiss any alternative practices. I feel sorry for them, because they are missing the mystery in healing. But just as often, you hear people that practice alternative practices dismiss Western medicine. All answers are not found in drugs or surgeries, but don't throw the baby out with the bathwater. If my appendix bursts, I want an IV packed with antibiotics and the best surgeon available.

I will say over and over, "my plan was my plan," and you may have your own combination of treatments that will work the best for you. It may have more Western pieces to it, or it may have a greater piece of Eastern philosophy. No matter which way you choose to heal, the best plan will be the one that makes your immune system, your mind, your spirit, your emotions and your body, as strong and healthy as it possibly can be. Since I had no options on the Western front, it was easy for me to feel free to explore as many options as came to me.

I didn't just have a desire to read about the wheel as a young mother. I wanted to walk the wheel. I had heard about a wheel in Wyoming, so it became a part of a family trip. We saw a sign on a little dirt road in the mountains and started up this mountain. Now, to this day I don't know what went wrong, because I don't remember seeing a turn-off, but we climbed an old dirt road up that mountain with no guard rails, in a full-size van. We had a child in the back seat who was afraid of heights, and she let it be known that we were going to fly off the side of the mountain at any moment. It had been my turn to drive when we started to see signs that said, "GOVERNMENT AIR FORCE FACILITY" and "Do Not Enter Under Penalty of Arrest." There was no way to turn around without entering, and there was no Medicine Wheel being protected by the United States Air Force. Getting down the mountain was a challenge, and Jim decided the best plan was to walk our little scaredy cat down the mountain. I drove the van down, as the other girls were discussing if it was smarter to wear a seatbelt as you crashed down the side of the mountain, or if it was better to have your hands free to take the chance to fly out and land in a tree! By the time we had all gotten to the bottom of the mountain, even I was out of the mood to look for the medicine wheel.

Now my mind and my emotions/relationships got good marks, but my mind and my body were struggling. In my 20's, I took my first yoga class, and at about the same time, I also read a book that changed my thoughts about what is possible. "There is a River," by Thomas Sugrue, is about Edgar Cayce, who is often called "the sleeping prophet." Shortly after reading this book, I took my first hypnosis training. For 18 years, I had traveled this path, always learning something new, and some of the things I came upon were not for me, but many things seemed to prove that the truth in philosophies are all the same. The truth is, God is love, be kind, and don't judge others. I was always meeting people that were traveling in my same direction. Now, these fellow travelers came to me with their techniques. Smiling, I imagined the dragon was blowing fire to scare me. That dragon would be surprised.

Bullies

The stroke dragon is a bully that sets out to steal your words, your graceful movement, and your dignity. Only once before had I had a problem with a bully, and that was when I was a middle school student. We had moved to a new town, and although everything was going pretty smoothly, there was a boy who was bigger than I was. Every afternoon, he would come up to me as I stood in line outside ready to be dismissed, and say, "Well how are you today Gage?" and then he would take his fist and hit me in the upper arm as hard as he could. My response was to look straight at him and remain calm as I smiled. Then I would look away before he saw the tears in my eyes. I am sure I frustrated him, because I would not respond, and by not responding no one came to my aid. But I am very stubborn, and it seemed important to not respond until I could figure out what to do. My Dad noticed that I was being very careful with my arm, and when we were alone he asked me what had happened. Now rather than being stoic, I cried and showed him my very bruised arm. He asked what I had done about it; did I tell the teacher? I told him, "no" because I was the new kid, and didn't want to get the reputation as a tattle-tale. He asked if this was a mean kid, and I had to tell him through tears that he was popular and everyone liked him, and that I never saw him be mean to anyone but me. My dad then asked if I would like him to take care of it. And I did really think about it this before I said "no" to which he said, "That is fine but then you have to take care of it, because this can't go on; nobody ever has the right to hurt you." We sat there for a few minutes in silence until I looked up and said, "I don't know how to take care of it." Well, a few minutes later I was smiling and going off to bed with my plan ready. The next day when this unsuspecting young man came up to me and said, "How are you doing Gage?" I turned, smiled and jammed the point of my umbrella down on the instep of his foot. After that, we became very good friends.

Now I was facing a bully again, and this time he did things over and over that hurt me. My dad was not around to consult, but I had to defeat the bully. I was not sure how; I only knew there was no way I would give in. If I had one piece of advice about how to heal, it would be just that - stay strong, face what is going on, and don't let the bully scare you! You don't need the whole plan all at once, you just need to keep doing the next best thing.

Spirit

Where should I start walking this wheel of healing? It seemed obvious my body is what needed the work. My Mind, Spirit and

Relationships were strong. I was very weak, so although each area touches the others, I needed to draw strength from the areas that were strong. So I would start with Spirit and Relationships.

Chief Seattle said it best when he said, "Humankind has not woven the web of life. We are but one thread within it. Whatever we do to the web, we do to ourselves. All things are bound together. All things connect." We often think of our place in nature when we read this, but it also can refer to our life in general. If one area is broken, it affects everything else. It seemed to me that the best way for me to fix my body was to engage my Spirit.

When I ask people to rate Spirit in their life many people will say, "I am not religious." My thought is, Spirit may have nothing to do with religion, although it can have a lot to do with religion. Spirit is what makes your heart sing; it makes life worthwhile. Spirit is good and just, it is kind and loving, it is what we came from and what we return to.

Many people call this God, but I don't know if it matters what you call it. I am betting the Supreme Being doesn't have an ego. Water is still wet no matter what you call it. In the last count, there are 7 billion people on the earth, and 95% believe in some higher power or Supreme Being.

Religions have differences, but in every Spiritual text we are told simple truths that are the same. Everyone's faith tells that God is love, we reap what we plant and we should not judge. I wonder what would happen if we focused on the similarities rather than the differences. There is a wonderful book by Marcus Borg called, "Jesus and Buddha: Parallel sayings." On one page is a saying of Jesus, and on the other, almost the identical saying of the Buddha.

I attended Winnebago Lutheran Academy for my high school education. It was a wonderful time for me, and I created a very strong base of what was important to me there. It was also a time when I started a life-long passion of the study of comparing religions and searching for the similarities in what other people believed. I could not understand how, if the premise was true, you must believe one thing to go to heaven, that same God could be called just.

I questioned that belief in religion class as a 17-year-old, and I wouldn't let the question go until a very conservative professor asked me to leave the class and go to the principal's office. The principal was a wonderful and wise man. He looked at me sternly, and after I told him the story and my questions he said, "First, you were disrespectful to disrupt a class. In the future, ask your questions after class, or you can come to me with whatever you are questioning." Then he very gently looked at me and said, "God comes to each of us in our own way. As Christians, we believe that the Bible is the Divine Truth, but we also believe that there is truth written on each of our hearts. You will learn to understand God in your own way and what he expects of you."

That thought made me want to understand what other people thought and believed. Now I could google every different religion, and I think there is probably a spreadsheet making it all very clear. At that time, the option was to read books about world religions, and I decided a good place to start was the Jewish faith. I often wonder what the rabbi thought when he looked up and saw a teenage girl, sitting in the back pew with a cheerleading sweater on, from the local high school. What I heard was kindness as he chanted prayers, and I felt a similarity to being in my own church.

Dalai Lama

Years later along my path of finding Spiritual sameness, I heard on the morning news that the Dalai Lama would be in Madison at the Buddhist Retreat Center, Deer Run, which is about 60 miles away. I wanted to see this great Spiritual leader's eyes and feel the presence of his energy, so I called and asked if there was a place I could stand to see him coming or going from one of his meetings. I was told he was only coming to do work at the University.

Wisconsin has the very good fortune of having the world-famous neuroscientist, Richard Davidson, who created the Center for Healthy Minds at the University of Wisconsin Waisman Center. Dr. Davidson had been studying the Dalai Lama, along with the Tibetan Monks, because of their ability to meditate. I have heard that when the Dalai Lama is being studied, and they remove the EEG leads, the energy remains on the screen until he is out of the building and two miles away. Most people still have a reading only until they get to the door.

Again, I asked if anyone could direct me to a door so that I could just see him, and again I promised I would not try to touch or talk to him. Yes, yes, I do understand that I sounded like a stalker. The woman on the phone seemed to understand my intention, or wanted to get rid of me, but she said that he would be coming to the convention center only to meet with the local Tibetan people. She told me I could see him come into the small gathering. I woke Gina up and told her to get ready - no school - we were going on a field trip, and we were off.

We got to the Center and Tibetan people were entering with their beautiful outfits, and Caucasian people were coming out. We went in only to be told that this was only for the Tibetan people. Once again I told my stalker story, and they waved me aside and said they would try to find the person that talked to me. They found the person that said I could stand in the hallway, however a few minutes later we were told to stand near the door; we couldn't stay in the hall. That lasted for a short time until the door had to be closed, and we were herded into the back of this small room filled with all the colors and sounds of a foreign land. I felt like Spirit was at my back, a gentle wind pushing me closer whispering, "This is what you requested, enjoy."

Someone motioned to me to come and fill the two empty chairs in the third row, right in front of the Dalai Lama. I was sure she was motioning to someone else, but as she persisted, I let her eyes pull me forward. The room was filled with color and tiny bells. He only spoke in Tibetan, and I do not speak that beautiful melody, but I was close enough to see his eyes sparkle; I heard his joyous laughter and felt the love he felt for his people, perhaps all people. After he left, I asked the little girl next to me, who was perhaps 10-years-old, if she could tell me what he said. She looked at me in disbelief and said, "You don't speak Tibetan?" I assured her that I did not, and then she asked if I had read any of his books. I told her I had read all his books to which she said, rolling her eyes a bit, "He always says the same old stuff - compassion-kindness-forgiveness and joy! You know, that same old stuff!" She was off to join her friends, the tiny bells on her dress announcing her departure. This is a very special spiritual memory for me. Buddhism is not a religion, but a way of life.

Now my desire would be to see Pope Francis.

Spirit is not captured by religions or ways of life. It is everywhere we look, and an equally spiritual feeling is possible in the space I meditate in my house, sitting on my steps looking at my picture of a kind smiling Jesus, or in a Chapel, Cathedral or Synagogue, or in the presence of the Dalai Lama.

I love the saying I saw recently, "Religion is a man sitting in church thinking about a kayak, and spirituality is a man in a kayak thinking about God." It really doesn't matter where you talk to God, because God is wherever you are. I guess whatever floats your boat, so to speak.

Spirit can be found where you least expect it. In a very strange set of circumstances, I found myself at a facility where there was an orangutan that had been raised by humans until they were old and no longer able to care for this exotic animal. They had surrendered him to the facility. The problem was the animal's anxiety level was too high for him to be in a cage with people looking at him without the clothes he had worn as he grew up with his family. The animal was very well treated and lived in a large area that was barred off from a meeting room. I was left to wait in this room and told not to touch anything or move, and they would be right back for me.

The orangutan walked into the room and we were separated by bars. I was drawn over to the bars, and he put his hand up, and I did the same. Our hands were so similar in everything but size. Now, as we stood looking at each other, he put his hand out, and hypnotically I handed him mine. He pulled me close and kissed my head.

Yes, I understand this was not the best safety practice; he could have reached out and killed me as easily as he had gently touched me and kissed my head. But I will never forget it, and in the last minute of my life, during the final review, it will be one of my best and most spiritual memories. I felt so deeply inside of me that we are truly all a part of the web. It is fear and greed that make us forget love, but there is no doubt that we are all connected no matter what culture or species we belong to.

God

I don't think that God is an old man sitting on a cloud with a naughty and nice list. I don't think he sends a thunderbolt of misfortune down on us if we are bad, or magical, wonderful luck if we are good. It says in the Bible that it rains on the righteous and the unrighteous. The stroke did not happen because I did something bad; it happened because, for some reason, my arteries are formed wrong. Stuff we don't like is going to happen to all of us. But sometimes it is there to make our life better. Many doors opened to me because of the stroke. I surely didn't see a blessing in the stroke at first; I only saw work, but that was the time that it was wise to follow the Jewish teaching that says no matter what happens to you, immediately say "thank you." This belief is that there is a gift hidden in every misfortune.

I felt God when I was touched by one of his amazing, wild animals, and when I heard the Dalai Lama laugh, but I also feel God when I hear Jim sing next to me in church, and when I think about the miracle of a single fertilized cell developing into a body and a brain filled with a hundred billion neurons. That these cells that are pure potential and can become humans is amazing. When you see a musician playing or singing with wild abandonment and joy, it is possible to believe they are creating with the Great One. Have you ever gotten so lost in creating, until someone wakes you from your trance? You may feel Spirit when you watch a sunset, or see the beauty of an athlete. But you can also feel the presence when you are sad or in pain. God is love, and God is in all things. You can feel it in sunshine after a cold winter, or a breeze that touches your skin. In Hebrew it is called "*shekhinah,*" which means light.

There is a poem in the ancient Welsh text, "The Black Book of Carmarthen," and quoted in "Celtic Fire," and edited by Robert Van De Weyer:

"I am the wind that breathes upon the sea,
I am the wave on the ocean,
I am the murmur of leaves rustling,
I am the rays of the sun,

I am the beam of the moon and the stars,
I am the power of the trees growing,
I am the bud breaking into blossom,
I am the movement of the salmon swimming,
I am the courage of the boar fighting,
I am the speed of the stag running,
I am the strength pulling the plow,
I am the size of the mighty oak,
And I am the thoughts of all people,
Who praise my beauty and grace."

Angels

There are many stories about angels that are sent to save people. There is the story of Daniel in the lion's den. The angels came and saved him, but we don't have to travel back so far in time. There is a story about a grandmother that lifted a car off her grandson, and she reported that there was someone there to help her. There is a good story about an old man in 1924 who had been in WWI. During this war he lost one eye, and the other was severely damaged by mustard gas. Now this old man, known as Pere' Jean Lamy, was walking down a country road, and he didn't hear or see two young men on bikes speeding along. Just before the first bike hit Pere', an angel appears. This angel picks the bike up a few feet in the air, by its two wheels, and sets it down gently in the grass. The second bike squeals to a stop, and the boys become very excited saying over and over, "There were two of them," meaning angels. Lamy was the very beloved village priest. It seems there were many incidences where divine aid had occurred when he was around.

There is a very good book by Doreen Virtue called, "The Angel Therapy Handbook," that tells the specific jobs of certain angels. The word, "angel" comes from the Greek and is translated as, "messenger of God." Archangels are the most powerful messengers. The Bible names Michael and Gabriel specifically, but Revelations speaks of seven archangels. The Jewish Talmud in the book of Enoch speaks of Michael, Metatron, Uriel, Gabriel, Raphael and Raguel. And in the Muslim Quran we hear about Michael, Raphael and Azrael. Some ancient writings talk about 15 Archangels.

Here are some of specialties of each of those angels:

Ariel - helps with nature issues, animals and the environment. This angel will also help with your material needs.

Azrael - People that are grieving belong to Azrael. This is also the angel that helps people cross from this world to the next, so I guess we will all meet Azrael someday.

Chamuel - We should all be talking to Chamuel, because his job is universal and personal peace.

Gabriel - If you are a parent or want to be a parent, call on Gabriel. He delivers clear messages, like he did when he told Mary about Jesus. He also helps teachers.

Haniel - This angel helps women with physical and emotional issues. He also helps with the gift of intuition.

Jeremiel - If you are trying to decide what to do with your life, and you are reviewing your past, this is the angel for you.

Jophiel - This angel cares about beauty. She also creates beautiful thoughts. If you are feeling down or are having negative thoughts, call on Jophiel.

Metatron - If there is a computer geek angel, this is it. He works with sacred geometry, those patterns in nature that we see everywhere. He is a good angel to help with time management and universal energies.

Michael - This is the rock star of the angels, the head honcho with his sword of blue light. I think we can assume he had the original lightsaber. Michael is all about protection. He brings courage to soldiers, firemen and policemen. But he also gives confidence, life purpose and safety to all that ask. Many people wear a medal to remind themselves that they are not alone but have help.

Raguel - She is the peacemaker and brings harmony to arguments and misunderstandings.

Raphael - Now Raphael has a big job in the healing arts. He helps the healers of both people and animals. He also watches over travelers.

Raziel - This angel is a bit secretive. If you have a dream you want to figure out, or contemplate the secrets of the Universe, Raziel is your angel.

Sandalphon - He is a special angel for musicians, and he is the mailman for the rest of us, taking messages between God and humans. I guess he does this in case you are having trouble connecting on your own.

Uriel - This is another angel that deals with intellectual pursuits, like writing, speaking, learning ideas and taking tests.

And **Zadkiel** - He is an angel who works with students, helping them remember facts and figures. He also helps us heal painful memories with forgiveness.

There are not only Archangels but hosts of angels. Most people who believe in angels also believe that we each have one or two guardian angels. A group of Native Americans believe that we have 49 angels. Seven angels are on duty at a time. Maybe those people deal with small children or are the dare-devil type. It seems like a good idea to always have fresh angels for that group. There is a Jewish saying that every blade of grass has an angel that says "Grow, grow." Which brings us to fairies, which many cultures believe are angels.

What I am about to tell you is one of those good news/bad news things. We have free will - that is the good news. We are allowed to change our thoughts and our beliefs, which in turn change our lives.

And there are Angels there to help us do the impossible. If Michael is helping your sister, he is free to help you too, because angels don't have any of those time and space limitations. And all of that is very good news. The bad news is the archangels will not dismiss your free will, so even if they can see you need help, and even if you are spiraling down into a whirlpool of negativity and Jophiel is watching you and wanting to help you, she won't step in until you ask. Angels are talked about 108 times in the old testament and 165 in the new testament. They are talked about in every spiritual tradition, so ask for help; they are ready and waiting.

Humans Doing Angel Work

What would the world look like if we all believed that each human was really light and love? Way back in the old testament we are told in Ezekiel 36:26-27, the Lord says, "I will put my Spirit within you." There is a wonderful quote by Wayne Dyer, "We are not humans on a spiritual path but spiritual beings on a human path." What if we really believed that, and when that spiritual flame in us tells us to touch another of these fellow spiritual beings in kindness we responded. Can we become a human doing angel work?

Two of these human angels may have saved my life. The first angel was an old Grandma in our town known as Mrs. Smith. On this day I was in our little grocery store. Because I was out in public without a straight-jacket, and everywhere I looked there were things that I could throw or break, I was holding my arm to my body. The claw decided to create searing nerve pain throughout my arm in protest. I bent down and pretended to read the back of a box, hiding my eyes full of tears that threatened to spill over no matter how hard I squeezed the web between my thumb and first finger. At that moment, I felt waves of hopelessness, and I wanted everything to be finished. I had no strength to do all the work of healing, and I was frustrated that I was unable to lift anything that weighed more than two pounds. The idea of death seemed easy and very welcome. I felt no reason to stay here. My motivation had been to stay because of Jim and the girls, but now I felt like was only a problem. Perhaps it was time for the 2nd escape clause. Oh, your mind can lead you down a very slippery slope, and if something doesn't stop you long enough for you to reframe your thoughts, who knows where that slope leads?

This is when Mrs. Smith stopped behind me and put her hand on my shoulder and said, "You only need as much faith as a mustard seed." Now, for a parochial school kid, that was pure comfort. I could do that; I knew how small a mustard seed is, and I believed the promise.

There was another day that nothing was going right; I couldn't focus on anything, words made no sense and I was seeing double. My arm and leg hurt, and I stumbled. Most of all I felt useless--like I was a problem for everyone. I was tired and at the same time felt restless. After numerous attempts to change my thoughts and mood, all to no avail, I walked out to the mailbox. I found an envelope with a small piece of paper inside from my cousin Tim. He was an optometrist, and on his prescription paper he had written these words, "Fear Not the Lord is with you! Cousin Tim." I smiled, went back into the house, crawled under my quilt, and imagined Jesus holding me. The Bible tells us 365 times to not be afraid.

Once I healed, I created CD's for my clients. They are called my "Fear Not's" and they are Bible verses that make me feel brave. When you have a history with scriptures, they are a real comfort.

Memorizing

There is a study that was done by the University College London, on London taxi drivers, and they found that these drivers, especially the ones that had been on the job the longest, had a larger than normal hippocampus (the hippocampus deals with long-term memory and spatial navigation), because they memorized the layout of the city and all of the streets. The study showed that the more we memorize, the more a part of our brain continues to grow. But this fact was not known during the 1960's when I was in high school. I wonder what this means to all of us, now that we memorize less and less, because of the convenience of our modern technology.

I remember being in school and being irritated by the amount of memorization that was required of us. We memorized in German Class and Latin Class; we memorized poems in English class, and in religion we memorized hymns, prayers and Bible verses. The theory was that we were training our minds. One of the teachers couldn't get through a class without repeating his favorite saying, "Repetition is the mother of all learning." However, I remember very clearly when someone groaned about another long assignment to memorize a psalm, we were quieted with a stern stare and these words were prophesied very quietly, "Someday you will be in a situation when words you have learned here will comfort you, strengthen you and bring you peace." Even as a teenager, it sent a cold chill down my spine, and I never forgot those words. Certain words did comfort me. It is very amazing when we look back at the long road of our life and see all the signposts that we have been given but didn't understand at the time. I received a signpost when I was 12. Each of us had a Bible verse chosen for us, and mine was Isaiah 40:29-30, "He gives strength to the weary and increases the power of the weak. Even youths grow tired and weary, and young men stumble and fall; but those that hope in the Lord will renew their strength. They will soar on wings like eagles; they will run and not grow weary, they will walk and not be faint."

It seemed way too long to memorize as a 12-year-old, but I underlined it in my Bible and learned it. You can imagine my surprise when the same verse was chosen for me at my high school graduation four years later. Maybe Kierkegaard said it best when he wrote, "We understand our lives backwards but we must live them forwards." I would put my babies to sleep with the song, "Amazing Grace" or "What a Friend we have in Jesus," but deep down I am grateful that my faith was deeper than that. I was going to need the comfort of the words I was forced to learn 30 years before the stroke.

Prayer

Prayer is being studied scientifically, and as humans there are many of us who want facts and figures - proof that it works. I was grateful that so many people were praying for me, but I have to admit facts and figures are interesting to me too.

San Francisco General Hospital was one of the places where research was done on how prayer affected 393 cardiac patients. Half of the patients were prayed for by strangers who only had the patients' names. The patients that were prayed for had fewer complications and less pneumonia; they needed fewer drugs, got better quicker, and left the hospital earlier.

There are many places that are studying prayer, but it is difficult to study, because it is a rather subjective study. Think of all the variables you would have to control. Does it matter how deep the faith was in the person that was praying for the patient? Does it matter if it was a Catholic prayer including a saint or two, a protestant minister, a person in prison or a monk? Does a prayer where you ask for your own healing work better, or is one where someone is asking for you more powerful? According to the research, none of it matters.

Faith, I think, is like mailing a letter. The prayer is the letter, and once you send it out, you don't keep wondering if the postman will drop it or if it will get there. You just trust it will be received.

Dan Buettner, a National Geographic explorer of people, found out in research for his book, "The Blue Zones," that the United States only has one Blue Zone, which is defined as a place where a group of people lived for over a 100 years and were still active, mentally alert, and had a generally good quality of life, and that was in Loma Linda, California. This group of people belong to the Seventh Day Adventist Church. They pray, but they also eat right, exercise and have a wonderful support system.

Maybe prayer is so important because we know people care, and perhaps it is the love that heals. If people pray for us, we know we are not alone, and if you don't have an earthly support system, you have a heavenly one. My daughter, Gina, wrote something for a college paper that rings true to me and is my prayer for you along your Spiritual journey:

"Whatever your connection to religion, I hope it provides comfort and warmth to you in times of trouble, guidance when the mind wanders to hatred, strength in times of weakness, light in your darkest moments and love enough to know we are never alone in this world."

Spiritual Warriors

I believe that we each can improve our health when we strengthen our SPIRIT. There are many different ways to understand Spirit. Some people get comfort in Bible verses and others in a different way. But there is a very important rule for Spiritual Warriors - you can't whine!

And we all have a desire to whine and minutes of fear and a lack of belief - those "poor baby" moments. Go off by yourself (my bathtub works for me), set a timer and feel sorry for yourself or get angry. This works for any situation that you feel is unfair. Tell your little minion that faithfully listens to you whine, how unfair the situation is. Perhaps name him/her, because the poor thing has listened to a lot of disgusting things. My poor listening minion is called "Pearl, as in "poor pitiful Pearl." Give yourself 10 minutes and then take a deep breath, laugh at your drama queen attitude, and make a real plan that has no time for tears or drama.

You either believe that you are the Beloved Child of God, a child of the Universe, or you don't, and if you do, then whatever is happening right now will turn out, if you continue to do your best. You might not like it, and you may stumble, but you have faith that you will be taken care of and whatever happens is the best for you right now.

Einstein said it best when he said, "I think the most important question facing humanity is, "Is the universe a friendly place? This is the first and most basic question that all people must answer for themselves."

Chapter 5

WORRY

My sister, Jill, always quotes, "If you worry, don't pray and if you pray, don't worry." I think that is the real crux of faith. Unless we choose to be hypocrites, we can't say we believe in something bigger that cares for us, and worry if he/she has the power to help us, or that we have the power to help ourselves.

There is an Old Irish saying that I have always loved:

Why worry? In life there are only two things to worry about:
whether you are well or whether you are sick.
Now if you are well there is nothing to worry about.
If you are sick there are only two things to worry about:
Whether you will get better or whether you will die.
If you get better you have nothing to worry about.
If you die you only have two things to worry about:
Will you go to heaven or hell,
and if you go to heaven you have nothing to worry about.
If you go to hell, you will be too busy
shaking hands with your old friends, that you will
not have time to worry!

Statistics

That saying can always make me smile, but Earl Nightingale, with the help of the Bureau of Standards, came up with these statistics for those of you that like statistics more than Irish humor.

40% of things you worry about will never happen.
30% are over and you can't do anything about them.
12% are needless worry about our health.
10% are stupid little worries.
8% are worth your concern.

Remember worry is using your imagination to create something you don't even want in the first place. I often hear people say things that make it sound like this is the worst time in history, and they are fearful, but we need to reframe that thought and put it in perspective. We don't have to worry about our future and live in constant fear. Times have always had unrest as far back as you want to go. The Civil War was possibly the worst time in our country, but WWI and WWII had fighting everywhere. Anyone that lived through the 60's and early 70's saw a fair share of unrest. President Kennedy was killed, and we watched it all on TV, and then we watched the Vietnam War on TV. It was the first war that was televised, and people reacted. President Johnson asked a group of the "wise men" of the country to get people behind the war. They suggested that people be given a more optimistic view on the progress of the war. Five days later, the President signed the Public Broadcasting Act, which allows someone to reframe the news. But even the "Wise Men" couldn't spin it for the group of people that rejected segregation, war, sexual mores, materialism and the lack of women's rights. Martin Luther King and Robert Kennedy were killed months apart. There was fighting in France and Mexico, and Russia had invaded Czechoslovakia. Three hundred students took over Harvard, and the National Guard was sent to many colleges to break up riots. Word of the My Lai massacre created antiwar riots in Baltimore, Boston, Chicago, Detroit, Kansas City, Washington and smaller cities. The bombings stopped, and the cold war heated up along with the politics at the Democratic convention in Chicago. There were the Black Panthers, the Chicago 8 and more riots. A U.S. plane was shot down over China, and President Nixon asked the silent majority to join him in solidarity toward the war effort and the draft. Instead, 500,000 people of that silent majority participated in a peace demonstration and marched in Washington D.C. People marched against war, the draft, segregation and for women's rights; they were arrested, pepper-sprayed and lynched in the south over voting rights. Detroit had the worst riot in American history. There were race riots, prison riots, and four students were killed and nine wounded at Kent State by the National Guard. The 60's were a time of real unrest.

I observed and questioned everything, making a very conservative professor pull me into the hall and state that in a year or two he expected that I would be a "rabble rouser" in Madison, making reference to the Sterling Hall bombing of 1965. In reality, I was more of a Simon and Garfunkel girl than Joan Baez and Janis Joplin. I chose to go to nursing school in Milwaukee, then became a rabble rouser in Madison. I lived with a black girl that became more of a sister than a friend, and civil rights became real. I dated a Vietnam War veteran, and the war was very real.

What does all this have to do with the story of healing? The times we live through create our beliefs. What we believe gives us power or makes us weak. I learned a few things during this time that became my belief system. Listen to both sides of an issue, but the best choice you can make is on the side of kindness and compassion. That includes compassion for yourself. I question anything that people say is the only way to do something, especially if they are making money on this "only way." I learned not to trust the broadcasting on TV as being 100% true. The closer something is to the earth in its simplest form, the better it is and DON'T BE AFRAID. There were frightening things going on, but so many wrongs were improving.

We each are responsible for creating a better world. So often you hear, "If God wants that to happen it will happen." It reminds me of a story about a man that was in a flood. Now this was a terrible flood with water spilling over the river bands and down the streets of the village. Pretty soon the water came into his house. He had moved everything to a higher level and felt safe until the water rose even higher. Finally, he climbed on to the roof of his house and hung on to the chimney, while he begged God to save him before the water reached the roof. A few minutes later, a neighbor came by in a rowboat and called out that he should climb down and be rowed to safety. The man looked at the water reaching the edge of the eaves and answered, "I am waiting for God to save me." The rowboat left, but a few minutes later a man in a pontoon came by and wanted to save the man clinging to the chimney, but he was told the same story, "I have prayed, and I believe if I am to live, God will save me." Then, when he had reached as high as he could, and the water was touching his knee caps, a rescue helicopter hovered over his house, and threw down a ladder, and still he answered the same way. The man drowned, and when he stood before God, he fell to his knees and asked "Why Lord, did you forsake me; how have I displeased you?" God looked at him and said, "I sent you a rowboat, a powerboat and a helicopter; I did not forsake you."

The Moslems have a great saying, "Trust God, but tie your own camel." There is also an old adage, "God helps those who help themselves."

My life was shaken up after the stroke, and sometimes that is okay. I would trust God, but I would do everything I could to heal, until he decided if I was staying or going.

90 Seconds

Fear is a one of two emotions we experience. You may think you have many more emotions than just two, but all other emotions are either a result of fear or love. Anger is fear of losing something or someone. According to neuroscientist Jill Bolton, it takes 90 seconds for an emotion to go through our system, sending all the neurochemicals cascading into tiny dishes on the top of the cells creating our feelings. If you feel anger, count to 90, and imagine the feeling floating away. We often keep hitting that fear or anger button, triggering it again and again.

My sister, Jill, is a spiritual warrior. All three of her sons were in different branches of the military and were involved in the Afghanistan/Iraq war. Any mother would tell you that the middle of the night is a hard time when you are thinking about a child. Those scary thoughts would rise out of her subconscious mind, and rather than think about the worst things that could happen, she would think of each of her sons and send them love. Then she would imagine a computer screen with the words "peace" and "love" in different colors and designs, moving all over the screen. She would do this until she fell back to sleep. She is a spiritual warrior, and she won that battle.

There was a study where a mother rabbit and a baby rabbit were separated. When the baby rabbit was caused stress, the mother rabbit became very agitated. They were in different parts of a building, but the cells knew. We are connected to our parents, kids and siblings on a cellular level.

There is a wonderful study involving heart cells. A man was at Walter Reed Hospital, and some of his heart cells were taken to Baylor Hospital in Texas. When he was stressed in Washington D.C., the heart Cells in Texas expressed the stress.

Do you have any thought that everything is not connected?

How do we become a Spiritual Warrior? Luke Skywalker and Harry Potter didn't become a Jedi or a Wizard by just wanting it, and neither will you. There are wonderful tools that you learn along the way, and they must be practiced. Remember, repetition is the mother of all learning.

Training your mind is a major practice in every discipline. These trainings affect you both mentally and physically.

Meditation

This is what I have learned when I think of changing your brain. Yes, you can actually change the structure of your brain when you meditate, along with relaxing your body, which decreases your pain and lowers your blood pressure. When you are able to affect your autonomic nervous system, your body is able to heal itself much more effectively. There are monks that have trained for many years and can control their minds and bodies. They can be in a 50-degree cave wrapped in a wet towel, and they can dry the towel by increasing the heat of their body. I realize that there are women out there in the midst of a hot flash who are thinking, "I can do that too," but in your case, think how good it would be to be able to cool a hot flash with cooling thoughts.

Meditation doesn't just work on our body, but meditation helps our mind too. It also helps the whole world. There was a study of

Transcendental Meditators done in Israel in the 1980's, during the peak time of the war with Lebanon, and reported in Yale's, "The Journal of Conflict Resolution." A few things happened as the TM meditators held the feeling and thought of peace; auto accidents and crime dropped, while the stock market went up 7%. The mood of the people went up 27%. The meditation classes improved and at the highest numbers, it started to affect Lebanon, and the war deaths decreased by 76%. It was figured by statisticians that the probability that all this happened by chance would be 1 in 10,000.

With meditation or self-hypnosis, you go into a place of focused concentration. During some types of meditation, you allow your mind to think of nothing specific, which reduces stress. The mind slows down to 7-10 cycles. Richard Davidson did studies with monks using brain imaging, and he found that the brain neural circuits change after practicing meditation. The area of our brain that is judgmental decreases, and the area of the brain that has been called the circuits for spiritual consciousness or neurotheology increases, and that creates inner peace.

Jon Kabat-Zinn says, "Meditation is neither shutting things out nor off. It is seeing things clearly, and deliberately positioning yourself differently in relationship to them." Another wonderful Jon Kabat-Zinn saying is, "You can't stop the waves but you can learn to surf."

Prayer is often meditative, and sometimes people go into that same neuroethology brain area. The difference is like the Diana Robinson saying, "Prayer is when you talk to God; meditation is when you listen to God."

The difference between self-hypnosis and meditation is that you use hypnosis to change something in your life. You go into that quiet place, and then you repeat a phrase, called an affirmation, or you imagine a picture to create new neuro-pathways.

For either of these meditative practices, you start by getting comfortable, but not so comfortable that you put yourself to sleep. Focus on something. Your breath is wonderful to use to focus, because you always have it right there with you! Take a nice deep breath, pushing your belly out as you breathe in through your nose, and imagine breathing in peace, joy, health. Then when you exhale through your mouth, pull your belly in. This takes some concentration, so your conscious mind is busy. Or you can count slowly up to 20 and then 20 down to 1. If you are meditating, you may just sit, touch each finger saying, "Saa, Taa, Naa, Maa," and when a thought pops up, think of it as a cloud or a wave and watch it go away. You can tell yourself that you will think of that later. If you are going for self-hypnosis, you may go to your favorite place. Create a place that is real to you, use all your senses until you can see the place in your mind's eye.

These practices are like rebooting your computer. It is good to shut things down, because everything works better when you turn it back on. People that use meditation or self-hypnosis tend to see results and become zealots. But for many people, the thought of meditation becomes overwhelming, and it becomes one more thing they have to do. One more thing they don't have time to do. I think perhaps we over sell it because it is really so simple. You don't have to sit cross-legged. The goal is to get into the "zone." We have all been there; it when you may be doing something and suddenly time seems to stop.

My husband Jim would not say he was a meditator, but he is. He is a bow hunter. He can sit in a tree quietly for three hours with no problem. Once I asked him what he thought about as he sat there, and he looked so quizzical and said, "Nothing." In the future, gentlemen, the best answer is always, "Why you my darling wife," but in this case it was the right answer because he had proved to me he was in the zone, allowing his mind to relax, recharge and refresh.

Mindfulness

And there is mindfulness, which is often thrown into the same category as the other three, because it is relaxing and therapeutic. Mindfulness is a way of life. This makes it even healthier for you, because it isn't something you carve time out for; it is how you live. When you are mindful, you stay in the moment which also reduces stress. When you are mindful you ask yourself, "What am I hearing right now? Smelling? Seeing? What is touching my skin or my taste buds?" When you feel anxiety or pure panic sneak up you, ask yourself, "Am I okay right now?" Because in truth, "right now" is all any of us have.

Start with mindfulness, which is very good for any anxiety or panic attacks.

Everything fits together, the mind affecting the body, and the spirit affecting the mind. Relationships affecting everything. It reminds me of a Jimmy Buffet song called "Fruitcakes." I think it is a good take on relationships. He says, "We all got them, we all want 'em. What are we going to do with "em?" and "But the right word at the right time may get me a little hug. That's the difference between lightning and the harmless lightning bug."

Chapter 6

THE BRAIN

The brain is formed after the heart, but it starts to grow from the bottom up. So, the first part that is formed is the brainstem, which regulates the physiology of the body. Next, the emotional parts of the brain, like the amygdala, are formed. The amygdala has the job of processing the emotions like fear, anger and pleasure.

This part of our brain is all about survival; it wants to keep us safe. So it plays the match game with everything that happens to us. Next, it decides where to store that experience. Let's say you fell down and got hurt as a little child, and you were given a cookie and told that it would make everything better. Maybe the memory gets stored together if there was enough emotion with it. Maybe you have heard the saying, "what fires together wires together." This is what it means when the neural pathway of being hurt and the pathway of the sweetness of sugar, get wired together. You get hurt anyway. Maybe this time your heart was broken and your body has a great desire for the dopamine surge that goes with it. It may have nothing to do with an addictive agent like sugar, alcohol or tobacco. What if the same thing happens to a child, and these parents are more stoic and say, "shake it off?" Depending on the emotion connected, it may make a child think, "I get love and approval if I hold my feelings inside," so those are the neuro-pathways that wire together. Wouldn't it be wonderful if humans came with a book of directions? We could look at our own book, or that of our children, and say, "I understand our issues."

Many of us were taught when we took anatomy and physiology, that we were born with brain cells and we gradually lose some of them throughout our lives. Not a wonderful outlook for old age. Einstein was wrong when he said that we only use 10% of our brain. I think he was saying, "People, don't worry about all those cells dying; you were only using 10% of your brain anyway."

In the 1980's and 1990's, scientists started to find that the brain is not hardwired, but it changes with training. And not only can it change, but there is a process called neurogenesis, which means that our brain is creating new brain cells into old age. If we have a brain trauma, we can move function from that trauma area to another healthy area.

Lorenz and Park, the team from the Center of Brain Health at the University of Texas, says the brain is setup to constantly reorganize and recruit more brain tissue as we need them.

The best thing we can do for our brains is to create more scaffolding. It is just what you are thinking - it is like the scaffolding you see on the side of a house. The Nun's study shows what they mean. Since 1986, David Snowdon from the University of Kentucky studied a group of Nuns. The Sisters were from Notre Dame, and they were tested throughout the years. They made a deal that after they died, their brains would be donated to the University to be studied. Sister Bernadette was a part of the study. She was interested in many, many things and she passed the cognitive tests with flying colors, until she died at 85 from a massive heart attack. In his book, "Aging with Grace," Dr. Snowdon writes, "... little doubt that Alzheimer's disease had spread far and wide. Tangles cluttered her hippocampus and her neocortex all the way up to the frontal lobe. The neocortex had an abundance of plaques as well." Even though Sister Bernadette rated a 6, the most severe rating for Alzheimer's, she lived a good, cognitive, fulfilling life. This has been replicated a number of times. Scaffolding is the process of building more and more neuropathways in our brains, and these are created by our thoughts. The more we think something, the deeper that pathway gets. Again, this is the good news/bad news scenario. If we are thinking good things and cementing the pathway in with actions, the pathway will be deep. Sister Bernadette was always learning something new, so she had many pathways and could move the information from one place to another. Music is a very powerful way to create scaffolding, because it integrates the whole brain. Music and singing are connected to our emotions; we hear a song and we may feel happy or sad. Music has the ability to improve our intelligence, creativity, and memory. Learning a new language and memorizing poetry both create scaffolding.

This picture of the brain may help you understand the brain a bit more.

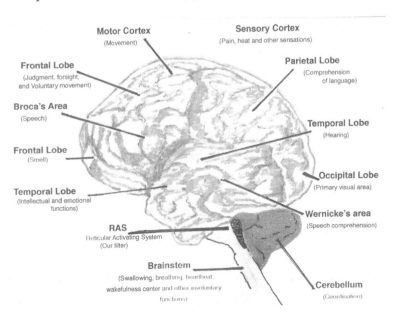

The brain is a three-pound organ that affects everything. Sometimes we act as if the brain and the mind are the same thing, and they are not. The brain is an organ that is found in the skull. You can touch it and take pictures of it, because it is a physical object. The mind, on the other hand, is abstract and can be found in our brain, but it is also in every cell in our body and includes the emotions.

Here are a few fun brain facts:

1. Your brain weighs half as much as your skin.
2. It is made up of 75% water.
3. There are 100,000 miles of blood vessels in the brain.
4. 60% of your brain is made up of fat.
5. Your brain uses 20% of the oxygen and 20% of the blood circulating in your body.
6. Excess stress changes your brain's function, its cells, and even the brain structure.
7. People are estimated to have 60,000-70,000 thoughts a day, but only about 1,000 of those are new.
8. Every sense has a corresponding physical place in the brain.
9. Music lessons in both children and adults increase the ability of the brain's organization and function.
10. A study that showed people who learned to juggle changed their brains in as little as 7 days. When we learn something new, it is good for the brain. I have had the greatest desire to learn to juggle since the stroke. Maybe it is my brain telling me that it would be a good way to heal and change my brain. I can see myself juggling as I do a stress management class. Maybe not five balls, but three would be nice. Once in Clearwater Beach, Florida, I saw a girl juggle fire and it was fascinating. My reason for wanting to develop this skill is the claw. People tell me all the time that they can't believe I have had a stroke and that it must not have been very

bad, because I have no lasting side effects. I smile and nod, responding that I am very blessed. The truth of it is, there are many side effects that I may be the only one that is aware of being "just a part" of me. Juggling is one of the things that make me remember and feel uncomfortable. When I try to juggle, the claw spins the ball off in one direction, not so much as you would notice in daily life, but my hand is not level, so the ball does not go where I mean it to go. The frustration causes me to stop practicing for a while and tell myself it is a silly childish endeavor. I know deep inside, that the day I can juggle three balls, I will be closer to being in control of my body.

In our brain, we have the prefrontal cortex, the conscious mind or the thinking part of our brain, that makes decisions and plans. Then, there is the limbic system, the subconscious or unconscious mind. The conscious mind is only about 10% of our brain. The subconscious mind or unconscious mind runs all of our 12 body systems. Think of how amazing it is that your body never takes a vacation, yet as long as you live it runs all these systems:

1. Integumentary (skin, hair and nails)
2. Skeletal
3. Muscular
4. Immune
5. Lymphatic
6. Cardiovascular
7. Urinary
8. Digestive
9. Respiratory
10. Nervous
11. Endocrine
12. Reproductive

When we think of the 12 systems that run our body, our life, how are we going to feed this living organism something that is better than any computer that could ever be created according to science at this time. It has been estimated, according to Greg Iles, that the brain has the storage capacity of six million years' worth of the Wall Street Journal.

When we think of what a healthy body can allow us to experience, we realize we need to nurture it. Each one of the 12 systems need nutrients and they can be found in whole foods - foods that are grown, not manufactured. Because I work with people with weight management, very often, I have studied many different diets. It seems to me everyone from the doctors promoting the Mediterranean diet, to Dr. Amen and Dr. Oz, are all basically saying the same thing in at least one aspect. Everyone says we need more vegetables; good fats for our brain, like nuts and avocados; and less meat. That is what Dan Buettner found in his National Geographic study of healthy people over 100.

Every study and doctor working with nutrition all seem to agree that processed food is not good for us, especially if we are healing from anything physical or emotional. Inflammation is both a problem in our body and a blessing. It is a blessing if you get hurt, because your immune systems send the right cells to that area to protect and start the healing process, but, it is bad if you keep hurting the same area over and over. Every disease has the common denominator of inflammation. By that, I mean everything from Alzheimer's, cancer, diabetes, colds, allergies, sinusitis, osteoporosis, arthritis and heart disease--every disease. Inflammation creates free radicals.

Knowing how we create inflammation is the first step in avoiding it. The number one way we create inflammation is with environmental toxins. According to the EPA, 2.5 billion pounds of toxic chemicals are being released by industries yearly, with 6 million pounds of mercury being released into the air.

Food

There are toxins on our food, but now the GMO's are also creating food sensitivities, because the toxins grow into our food as well. We clean our homes with toxins and apply toxins to our body's largest organ; our skin. Don't forget, one of the biggest ways that we create free radicals is stress.

> "Let food be thy medicine and medicine be thy food."
> **– Hippocrates**

There are ways we can turn our life and health around and become healthier mentally and physically.

1. We can eat antioxidants which are vegetables and fruits. We all know that these are good for us, and it is better if you get as many colors, especially dark colors, as possible. Some of the superfoods are berries and grapes, nuts and green tea, dark greens and orange vegetables like sweet potatoes, carrots and squash.
2. We can eat organic food when it is possible.
3. Reduce our sugar intake. The number one thing that causes free radicals to rust out our body is sugar. Sugar is everywhere, and according to the USDA, the average American eats 150-170 pounds of refined sugar a year. There are also things that turn into sugar in our body, like alcohol. Cancer needs sugar to live.
4. Start using natural cleaners like vinegar and baking soda, or natural essential oil cleaners, like Thieves, in your house.

And only use soaps, lotions and deodorants that you can pronounce on your body.

5. Drink good clean water. We need so much water, because every cell in our body uses water, and every function needs water. If you are not getting sufficient fluid, your reflexes are as slow as a drunk driver. Many experts say we should drink half the number of our weight in that number of ounces of water daily.

The body is 75% water and 25% matter.
Muscle is 75% water.
The brain is 75% water.
Bone is 22% water.
Blood is 83% water.

Water:

- Moisturizes the air in the lungs
- Water is a cushion for our vital organs
- Is needed for our metabolism
- Regulates body temperatures
- Moves toxins out of our body
- Helps to absorb nutrients and dissolve minerals
- Protects and moisturizes joints and tissues

Stress Management

6. Reduce stress, because it will kill you, or at the very least it will create a chronic disease or two in your body or mind. Here are five quick stress relievers:

A. Practice breathing slow, easy breaths, pushing your belly out as you breathe in through your nose, and in as you exhale through your mouth. Do this at least four times a day.

B. Be grateful. Remember you are not seeing the big picture, and most often everything works out, if you just take the next best step.

C. Quiet your mind; take time to relax. I like to use self-hypnosis, because I can do it in 2 minutes a few times a day.

D. Be mindful, by thinking right this minute, "Am I okay?" The military uses some- thing called HALT to take an evaluation of their emotions. HALT stands for, "Am I Hungry, Angry, Lonely or Tired?" It helps you to evaluate what it is that you really need. Then, you can say, "Everything is good with me. I am just tired. Right this minute I am good."

E. Lose weight! Two out of three Americans are overweight or obese. Every pound you lose takes 7 pounds of pressure off your knees and ankles. Your blood pressure and blood sugar levels improve too. Losing weight takes stress off your body which also heals your mind.

F. Stress comes when you let the "shoulds" rule your life. There is trouble when we try to live the way others think is right for us, rather than listening to our own heart. I love a song by folk singer David Roth called, "Don't Should On Me." In the lyrics he says, "Don't should on me, and I won't should on you." I think the stress level would decrease if we all followed that rule.

G. Laugh every day; find beauty and wonder. Be curious about life all around you. Lee Berk, from the University of California, said about the medical benefits of laughter, "If we took what we know about the medical benefits of laughter and bottled it up, it would require the FDA's approval." There is a wonderful book called, "Anatomy of an Illness," by Norman Cousins that talks about his illness called ankylosing spondylitis. Specialists said his chance of recovery was 1 in 500. Cousins left the hospital and laughed with friends and at books and movies. He found that 10 minutes of good laughter creates 2 hours of pain-free sleep.

H. Move your body, and get outside to walk and play. It can really improve the part of your brain called the cerebellum. This part of your brain deals with planning, goal setting, perception, coordination and time management. So how do you get more scaffolding in the cerebellum? You practice any exercise that uses fine or gross motor coordination, like playing a musical instrument or dancing, practicing a sport like tennis or golf, or doing martial arts or yoga.

I. Play the compare and contrast game. I will tell you about this little game I play. I used to think about how much easier and safer my life was than, say, a woman crossing the country in the early 1800's. Then I heard about Immaculee Ilibagiza. Her story is written in the book, "Left to Tell: Discovering God Amidst the Rwandan Holocaust." Immaculee was a college student in the Rwandan holocaust. Pastor Murinzi hid a great danger to himself and his family; six women in a bathroom that was four feet long by three feet wide. There was a shower stall at one end and a toilet at the other. There was not even enough room for a sink. Eight woman lived in this space for three months and often heard through the walls, the horror that was happening as the Tutsis killed Hutus in the most inhumane ways, while the women constantly lived in fear. Immaculee asked for a Bible and a dictionary and taught herself English in this time. When they were rescued by the French, they only had the clothes they had worn for three months. Immaculee went from 115 pounds to 65 pounds. All of her family and friends were dead, except for a brother away at college. She forgave the man that killed her family.

When I feel I am stressed, or I feel like life is unfair, I try to remember to think about Immaculee, and the stress runs away knowing that it was childish.

Heart

As wonderful as our brain is, the heart could be classified as spectacular. We have known for many years that the brain and the heart are in constant communication, but the scientific research that has come out since 1970 shows that the heart makes many of its own decisions. The ancient wisdom of yoga has told us that the heart is our center, and many belief systems think that the heart is where the soul is found. Proverbs 23:7 says, "For as a man thinketh in his heart, so he is." In Luke 5:22 it says, "What reason ye in your heart." But these same thoughts are found in the Jewish, Islamic and Hindu traditions as well.

The root word for courage is the Latin word, "cor," which means heart. Our cultural sayings reflect that it is the organ of our feelings. Think of all the references involving the heart:

- heart and soul
- broken heart
- follow your heart
- heart's desire
- heart to heart
- heart of gold
- man after my heart
- hardened heart
- heart of stone
- brave heart
- cross your heart
- bless your heart
- change of heart
- listen to your heart
- chicken heart
- have a heart
- let your heart rule your head
- their heart is in the right place

It seems that we always knew that the heart was the seat of the emotions, but we're just waiting for science to catch up.

Science knows these facts about the heart; it pumps about 100 gallons an hour, or two gallons a minute. This next fact is mind-blowing, because it is pumping this blood through about 60,000 miles of blood vessels. It is just about 25,000 miles around the earth, so the heart pumps the blood a distance of more than twice around the world. I am not saying it does this in your lifetime, but in 60 seconds it will have moved blood to every cell in your body.

The heart starts beating before the brain is even formed in a baby's body. It will be the last thing to happen before we are declared dead. Our brain can be dead, but our body will still have a heartbeat. When a heart is transplanted, all connections to the brain are cut, and it is placed into a new body. Surgeons don't know how to reconnect the heart to the new brain, but it doesn't seem to be a problem. The heart starts beating and functioning.

There was research done in the 1970's at the Fels Research Institute that says the brain can send a command to the heart, and the heart may or may not obey. It tends to use its own logic as to how it will respond. This is the amazing thing though; the heart sends a message to the brain that it fully understands and obeys. The Laceys, who did this research, say that the beat of the heart is a language that the brain understands. When we start to worry and let fear run through our brain, which is at odds with the heart emotions of hope, harmony, peace and joy, we create incoherence. If you were connected to a EKG and an EEG, you would see the wave patterns going in opposing ways, showing stress.

In 1996 Daniel Goleman published his book about emotional intelligence. The good thing about his findings is that while our IQ comes with us at birth, we can increase our EQ. The way we do that is to acknowledge the connection between our thoughts, feelings and the way we react. When our heart and our brain are in harmony, we are calm and every cell in our body is healthier. A way to do that is to use something called Heart Math. The Heart Math Institute, started in the 1990's, and gives ten techniques to create a way to listen to our heart.

My very favorite technique is called freeze frame. These are the five steps to freeze frame:

1. Recognize the stressful feeling.
2. Shift your racing monkey mind or upsetting emotion to your heart area. You can do this by putting your hand on your heart and breathing in as if you were breathing through your heart.
3. Think about a fun time that you have had in the past. Try to relive it using all of your senses.
4. When you are in a relaxed state, ask yourself, "What would be a better response to this situation?
5. Listen for your intuition

One day, I went to visit my great aunt and found her sitting on the sofa with the most beautiful smile, her eyes closed. I announced my arrival and asked what she was doing. She looked at me and said that she was going through her memories. I thought it was funny because I saw no albums and asked if she meant her pictures. She said no, that books and pictures could be lost, damaged or destroyed. But when something was really wonderful, and you were having a grand time, you should stop and think of it in detail, just as if you were taking a photo complete with all of your senses. Then, store it safely away and you can relive it anytime.

When I had enough energy to walk a little, I went to see my grandma who lived next door, just 300 feet away. I know that exercise is like a magic pill, and everything is better if we move our body, but I physically could not walk farther than that. My solution was to take a stick and lay it down on the side of the road and promise myself that I would walk at least three feet farther the next day. The next day I would move the stick again. Then, I started putting my hands on the top of my head and visualize a light streaming into my head from heaven. I would imagine this light reconnecting any of those connections in my brain that were broken. I often used visualization, because our subconscious doesn't know if something is real or imagined, and our body will react to our thoughts. Let me give you an example. Imagine that the person next to you has lice. I mean those jumping, fat little insects. When they jump into your hair and make a tiny nest for the new lice, it makes you itch! In fact, that is how you know you have lice, you feel the itching in your scalp. Another example is to imagine a really beautiful fat lemon. It is so full of juice that when you cut the lemon you see a little drop of lemon juice come to the surface. Then you take the half of that lemon and you bite into it and feel the juice fill your mouth. If you just felt your scalp itch, or your mouth fill with saliva, you created a physiological reaction with just a thought!

I was counting on my cells reacting to my thoughts. You can see that it is the pictures that our subconscious understands, and the more details you create with your thoughts, the better it works. My Dad worked with electricity, so it was something that was familiar to me as I grew up. After the stroke, I would think of a fuse box, and every time I couldn't think of a word, said the wrong word, or any of the hundred things that would go wrong, I would take a breath and imagine I had just tripped the fuse. I would literally touch my head and imagine that I was pushing the fuse button back. Every now and then, I would go to the fuse box and touch the fuse buttons and then touch my head and the imaginary fuses. This seemed to be a very effective way to give myself some sense of control.

More than just doing the visualization, I was also doing energy work on myself. Right after I started doing hypnosis on clients, I discovered that I could touch someone's hand while they were in trance and say a little prayer to myself that the right words would come to me that would help this person. I would also imagine that my energy was flowing into the other person. I would be exhausted after doing a few hypnosis sessions, but most times people would wake up and say, "Wow, that was wonderful - I feel great!" I was having a conversation with a reiki master and asked how they keep their energy level high, because I could see no more than four people in a day, and I could barely get home from being so exhausted. When I write this, I can't believe how egotistical it sounds. Why would I assume that my energy was something that would be good for another person? The reiki master was kind and didn't bring that piece up, but told me how I was hurting myself. So we met, and she and another reiki master did an attunement on my energy, and I started to study energy practices. I studied everything from reiki, to quantum healing, and therapeutic touch to access consciousness. What I found is; they all have different techniques, but for me they are all the same. There was a recent study that looked at many different disciplines and found the techniques utilized mattered just 17% of the time, the rest was the practitioner. I don't think one person is more magical than another. The way energy works may be magical, but it is more about who you resonate with. Who can you open up enough to that you can allow the magic to happen? Practitioners in all of these different practices understand that they are only a reed. All their negativity must go as they allow the energy to flow through them and into the person they are helping, with absolutely no expectation other than they are asking that healing energy flow into this person in front of them.

Over the years, all the things I have learned have melded together, and I feel energy in my own way. I studied all these different techniques in the same way I studied comparative religion. I read and listened to the masters, and then I searched for what was the same in each religion or energy work. When I identified that sameness, I decided that was my truth.

If you are interested in feeling energy, start by putting your hands about six inches apart and move them back and forth slowly, until you feel something push back. As you practice, it gets easier and easier. Another way that I feel it is easy to feel energy, is to put your hands up and move them back and forth about 6-8 inches away from the tree trunk. You will feel the vitality of the tree itself. This is really easy in the spring when the tree is coming to life.

In the book, "The HeartMath Solution," by Doc Childre and Howard Martin, they write, "Heart intelligence is the intelligent flow of awareness and insight that we experience once the mind and emotions are brought into balance and coherence through a self-initiated process. This form of intelligence is experienced as direct, intuitive knowing that manifests in thoughts and emotions that are beneficial for ourselves and others."

The Knowing

This knowing was something I had been familiar with since I was thirteen years old and every time I asked for it, I expected it to show up. I believed the Bible verse Matthew 7:7: "ask and it shall be given, seek and ye shall find, knock and it shall be opened unto you."

When I was 13 years old and finishing eighth grade, something rather strange happened to me, and it was my first experience with the "knowing" that I remember. My parents were not people who went to church every Sunday, but they always went at Christmas and Easter, and my mom managed to attend a few more Sundays. For the last two years, we had lived across the street from a Lutheran Church. My parents wanted all of us to be confirmed so that we had a foundation to build from what we believed. Thirteen miles away, there was a Lutheran high school. A couple of the people in my confirmation class went to Winnebago Lutheran Academy, and the rest to our local high school. I had every intention to attend the local high school. Then something happened. I can't say I heard a voice; it was more like what I call a "knowing." I knew I was supposed to go to WLA, so I talked to my parents who said, "No," because we only had one car that my dad drove to work, so how did I think I would get there? How did I plan on paying for it? Why would I even consider going there when there was a free school three blocks away? My family thought I was probably just having trouble at school with someone. I explained that it had nothing to do with my friends, I just knew it was something I needed to do. It is a bit hard to explain the knowing without sounding like a Joan of Arc wanna be, and you know how that turned out. I went to the Pastor who asked me why I had not taken the entrance test when it was offered. I called the school, and they set up a test at the church, found a ride for me, and talked to the financial aid office. My parents said as long as I had everything figured out, and I was sure that I wanted to attend, they were willing to pay the tuition. I had four wonderful years at a very good school.

The next time, the knowing came so forcefully, it made me stop and turn. I was going to college to be a teacher. It was a month before I was to leave for school when the "knowing" arrived. I was to go to nursing school. Now, I played "school" as a child, and I was the teacher. I thought that was the best path for me; in fact, the only thing I knew about being a nurse was from a novel I had read; "Cherry Ames Nurse," and a book I had read about Florence Nightingale. I argued my case, but the knowing would not retreat. But somehow, my RAS which seems to be best friends with the knowing, showed me everything it could about healing and nursing. I knew a friend of my mother's had attended Deaconess Nursing School in Milwaukee, so I called and was told by a very nice lady that they would put me on a list for the next school year. When I informed her I was planning attending the current semester in just a couple of weeks, she laughed. A week later she called and said, "You won't believe this, but someone dropped out, and everyone else on the list already has plans." I would believe it, and it made me understand Joseph Campbell when he said, "Follow your bliss and doors will open where there were no doors before."

It was not nursing that was my bliss, but the "knowing" itself is 100% pure bliss. It has happened a handful of times in my life. Sometimes on big things that changed my life, but more often in times that just brought me joy. I believe the secret to it happening is something the Buddha said, "Open to everything and attached to nothing." I wanted to live, but I was open to the ultimate adventure if that was what was meant to happen. The feeling when the knowing happens is that I am creating something with God. I see, feel or know what he wants from me.

Most of the time, I have expectations for myself, and I think I know what should happen, so I push to make it happen. The problem is that everything is a balance. If life is like a river, there are times you get to float, letting your thoughts drift like a summer day, floating peacefully. That is the knowing, but things happen in life, and we get caught up in stress, illness, sadness and the white waters of life. At those times, you need to put your back into it, and use all your strength to focus on the place you want to move toward. The knowing has never removed the rocks and the rapids. We need those times to get stronger and learn new things about ourselves. The knowing just makes you aware you are on the right path, and that you need not travel alone.

I walked with my hand on my head feeling the energy coming in and asking not for healing, but rather that knowing to come to me. My prayers were answered when I heard inside of me, "What do you want? Do you want to come home or stay?" It was like waking from a trance, real enough to make me stop and think, "I would like to stay if I can be of use to my family. If I can heal, I want to stay, if not I want to come home now." Then as quickly as this started it was finished, and I knew the healing was there. I also knew there would be much work to do, because I knew the end of the story. I expected that the answers would unfold as to how it was going to happen piece by piece in the exact way I could understand and use them.

I would like the story to end here and let you think that I was brave and strong enough to always trust and believe this great gift I had been given, but that was not the truth. Sometimes I forgot, and was so frightened thinking it was all happening again, and sometimes I slid into a depression thinking I never would be of any use to anyone. Often, despair was my friend when I wondered who I was now, and what my future was going to become. But from that day forward, I knew there was a rope I could reach for on the most difficult days.

Gratitude

I had a friend that had stage four cancer. The hospital sent her home, because they could do nothing more for her, medically. What they did do for her, was to give her a picture of the body and indicate the five places she had cancer. Places like her liver, brain and intestines, the big kinds of cancer. She threw the paper work on her table and went to bed. But in the morning, she looked at that picture, and she thought about the fact that it made up only 20% of her body. So that meant 80% of her body was working very well. If you have ever worked with a child or a pet, or tried to change a piece of your own behavior, you know it is better to focus on what is good and right. That is exactly what she decided to do. She thought about it, and she celebrated everything that was right with her health, and a miracle happened; the cancer went away. This amazing woman forgave everyone that had ever hurt or disappointed her, even herself.

Gratitude surrounded her like a fog; she was grateful for all 12 systems every day. She let go of self-limiting beliefs and looked for all the joy, beauty and love she could find. Then she started to teach others how to face their own dragons, and other people healed. Even oncologists came to her classes and lectures.

The cancer found a way to sneak back into her life after ten very productive years that were filled with humor and gratitude.

What would happen if before we got out of our beds in the morning, we told our bodies how very grateful we are for each of the twelve systems?

My mother taught me, as a very young child, the little poem written by Robert Louis Stevenson:

"The world is so full of a number of things, I'm sure we should all be as happy as kings."

But it didn't stop there. If we were complaining, she would say, "Can you see, did you walk in here on your own two feet? Do you have a roof over your head and food to eat? I imagine there are many people that would be happy to trade places with you."

My mother was a great advocate for gratitude, before anyone even thought of gratitude journals.

Many studies are being done about gratitude all over the world, and here are a few of the results:

Personality - you will find you are more optimistic and less materialistic. You will have higher **self-esteem** and make better decisions.

Your **health** is a big winner of being grateful. Sleep is improved, you have a better **immune system**, and there is a decrease in depression and blood pressure. You have more energy, less pain and live longer.

Emotionally - grateful people have more friends and better relationships.

Socially, people that practice gratitude are more relaxed, more resilient and kinder. That would be a good thing for all of us.

There was a study where someone did an act of kindness for another person, and both the person that was kind and the recipient of that kindness had an increase in their serotonin level. You could expect that, but the amazing thing that happened was that everyone that witnessed the act of kindness had an increase in serotonin as well, that wonderful feel good hormone.

Serotonin and endorphins are neurotransmitters that reduce pain and make us feel good. We can truly be grateful for the brain's ability to create chemicals that rival morphine in effectiveness. Every thought that we think creates a chemical reaction in our body. It is as if our brain has its own little pharmacy. You think a thought, and the chemicals are sent to every cell in your body. Then the chemicals cause you to experience pain or release the pain. You can feel happy and relaxed, or you can feel stressed and watch your blood pressure soar. What amazing bodies we have.

Before I go on, there is a difference between the brain and the mind. Remember the brain is a physical organ that can be touched, but our mind is not physical and is really in every cell. Buddhists believe that our body is like a guest house, and our mind is a guest that will someday move on.

The conscious part of our mind that deals with making plans just wants the facts. It is like that old TV show Dragnet and how the investigator, Sgt. Joe Friday, would say over and over, "just the facts ma'am." Now, those facts are really our perception, because facts are seen differently by each of us. Still, facts give the subconscious mind something solid to influence our choices.

The subconscious mind, which is much larger, deals with feelings, words, both the tones and frequencies of the voice, pictures, smells, and all of our memories. Think of it as a sponge with all those little holes and crevices. It stores everything that people say to us, along with everything we sense.

It makes you wonder how your brain delivers what it needs out of all this information. Some scientists estimate that if the brain was a computer, it would have several terabytes and several petabytes, which is a whole lot of memory. But other scientists say you can't even compare; you would need much more storage capacity in a computer, because we are storing data in a whole different way.

The RAS

There is a piece of our brain called the RAS or reticular activating system. This filter is found just above the brainstem. It is about as long as your thumb, and it is one of the most amazing things in your life.

Every minute that you are here walking around and living your life, you are being bombarded by two million pieces of information. You think you have trouble making up your mind now! We would be absolutely crazy if we had to deal with that much information. So this amazing filter system takes the two million bits of information and lets you be aware of 5-9 pieces, which in reality is still quite a bit, every second. Right now the RAS is being studied with the idea that perhaps ADD may be a result of letting too many of those pieces of information through, and dementia, too little.

This is the important part of all of this; the way that your RAS knows what to let through and make you aware of is what you are thinking about and what you are saying to yourself. Your subconscious just wants to make you happy, but it is a bit like Dr. Spock on "Star Trek," or Sheldon on "The Big Bang Theory." It is smart, but has no sense of humor. It definitely does not understand a joke, sarcasm or any words that you couldn't draw. That leaves the negative concepts out, so if you say, I don't want to be sick, broke, fat etc., your old RAS thinks that is exactly what you do want. It has 2 million ways to be sick every second.

If we decide we are going to get a red car, I mean we really desire a red car, and you think about it over and over, you will start to see red cars everywhere you look.

Your RAS is a wonderful servant if you train yourself to speak and imagine what you desire, rather than what you fear. But it is a terrible master if you are not in control of it.

There is an old Cherokee legend about a grandfather that knows his grandson is having some problems. So the grandfather tells the grandson there are two wolves that live inside of him and they battle. One is evil; he stands for anger, jealousy, regret, hatred, ego and resentment. The other one is good. This wolf stands for joy, peace, love, hope, humility, kindness, truth, faith and compassion. The grandson asks, "Grandfather, who is going to win?" The grandfather answers, "Whoever I feed."

It matters what we focus on. Whatever we focus on and think about grows. And we have our RAS to thank for that. RAS thinks we must want whatever we are spending so much time imagining. You see, we can imagine what we want or what we don't want. That is our choice.

Einstein said, "Imagination is everything. It is the preview of life's coming attractions."

The Fear Dragon

When I would wake up in the middle of the night, usually about three o'clock with the fear dragon strangling me, I would listen as he recited back to me all my fears - all the dire predictions of hyper-fibro-dysplasia. I heard how I was only a burden to my family and society as a whole. You see, the fear dragon is only digging out of you all your fears. You have the choice to believe them or not to believe them. I was familiar with all these negative thoughts, and they were of absolutely no help to me. Those thoughts had created a neural pathway in my brain and something that should have been one of those 8% "worth your concern" type of worries. You need to create a new pathway before those negative thoughts become a belief. Every time those thoughts pushed their way into my conscious mind, I would say to myself, "There is a reason I am supposed to be here, or I would have died. Now, what can I do this minute that is a wiser use of my time." What I decided to do if I couldn't sleep, the best use of my time was for visualization. As a hypnotist, it is one of my favorite ways that I believe people can change things in their life. The doctor had drawn me a clear picture. I would advise you to ask your doctor to draw you a picture of what is wrong in your body, and then find a picture of what it would look like if it was as it should be. My arteries should not be sucked together, so I imagined opening them. Now these pictures don't have to be amazing works of art, and if you ask your physician to draw for you, you may very well hear how many years they went to school, but never had an art class. Please believe me; it is important for your subconscious to understand what things look like. You can't imagine the number of people that I see who shake their heads "yes" when the doctor asks if they understand, and then later ask me what the doctor meant. I have very easy-to-understand books about our anatomy and what our joints, organs, muscles, nerves, vessels and bones are meant to look like when they are healthy. There is even a wonderful pop-up book. If you don't know, and I mean really understand, what is not picture-perfect in your body, how are you going to visualize the change?

Resilience

People that can cultivate this trait are not born to doing it. These people can deal with stress much more effectively, so they are healthier and enjoy life more.

Here are just a few examples of people with this personality type:

1. Bethany Hamilton was a 16-year-old surfer when a Tiger Shark bit her arm off at the shoulder. By the time she had reached the hospital, she had lost 60% of her blood. Three weeks later, she was back on her surf board trying to figure out how to compensate for only having one arm.

2. Aron Ralston, 28, was a rock climber. When he was climbing in the Utah desert, his arm was trapped under an 800-pound boulder. After a couple of days, he knew nobody was going to show up in time, so he amputated his own arm with his pocket knife. He still had to rappel down 80 feet and walk a few miles until he could find help.

3. And my personal favorite is Louis Zamperini, the World War II airman that had been shot down and lived on a raft

longer than was thought possible, only to be captured by the Japanese and put in a prison camp.

Al Siebert, the author of, "The Survivor Personality: Why Some People Are Stronger, Smarter, and More Skillful at Handling Life's Difficulties," says these are the traits of a survivor:

1. Acceptance
2. Optimism
3. Creative problem-solving

I think the octopus is the perfect image for resilience. Here are a few facts about octopuses:

- They are flexible in body and behavior
- They learn easily and can problem-solve
- They can remove a plug or unscrew a lid to remove prey from a container

- They can use tools (not a hammer or screw driver, they are not quite that cool, but they can use a shell and a stick-like object)
- They can hide from their predators in plain sight
- They have four pairs of hands - the envy of all mothers
- They have three hearts, which would possibly end wars if humans could duplicate that
- They have nine brains, which would definitely end wars if it was a human attribute
- They have been found to play with 'toys'
- When all else fails, they can lose a limb and regrow it with no permanent damage. Bethany and Aaron didn't grow new limbs, but there was no permanent damage to who they are.

We are born with the will to survive, but if we can learn to problem-solve with both sides of our brain, we will create a flexibility of thinking. The left brain is in charge of judging the situation that you find yourself in and then organizing solutions in your mind that would work. The right half of your brain deals with what you feel is the right thing to do, your intuition, the acceptance of the situation, and faith.

Brian Luke Seaward teaches ways to become more resilient in both his book, "Managing Stress: Principles and Strategies for Health and Well-Being," and in his Stress Management trainings. If you ever get the opportunity to hear him speak or take his trainings, I can't say more than, don't pass up the opportunity. His books, videos and films were an important piece in my healing. I met Brian Luke at the National Wellness Conference and took his week-long class in 2003 to become a stress management specialist. I was not working yet, but I took it on myself as part of my healing, and Brian Luke was a blessing, giving me tools in his compassionate, healing way.

Wedding

Becca and Eric were getting married Thanksgiving weekend, and it was going to be a big wedding. I was doing pretty good, smiling and pretending, but I was very nervous, because the panic attacks were strong when I was in a crowd. Now I was planning on hosting a crowd of 200 people with no place to hide. Granted, my conscious mind was a bit angry at me, because most of the people that were coming were people that cared about me. They were my family, but my subconscious mind could care less who they were. It was a group of people that were sucking up my oxygen, or whatever your twisted brain thinks, when you are in the midst of a panic attack.

Eric's family was from Kansas, and they came early to spend Thanksgiving with us, so we could get to know each other. We made it through, with me popping out of the room every hour or so for 10 minutes, so I could run upstairs and hypnotize myself. That would not be an option at the wedding.

This was the solution for me; when I felt a panic attack coming on, I was to get to Jim, or he would keep his eye on me, and if he saw the deer-in-the-headlights look he would come to me, and I would bury my head in his shoulder, and he would cover my ears. We looked like a very loving couple. I could shut everything out, and focus on his smell - a smell that is very familiar to me and comforting. With his hands on my ears, and my eyes covered on his chest, I could breathe for a few minutes and be okay again.

This is why children have a blankie and need it at daycare. The smell reminds them of home.

These challenges, like the wedding, were good for me, because it made me remember who I was and ignite my cell memory.

Becca, like Jim, seemed to see me as if nothing had changed, so the summer after her wedding, she called and asked if a friend of theirs from the Coast Guard could get married in our backyard. I said, "Of course," and asked how many people and she told me. I started to think about what we would need when she said, "Oh, by the way, they don't belong to a church, so they have nobody to marry them. Could you do that?" My thought was, "Not legally," but as she knew, I would think about it, and when I asked my old Pastor friend if he would help, he said he was going to be out of town, and he suggested I get an internet certification to marry people. I did just that, and it started a whole new piece of sharing in my life.

A month later, someone called and begged me to do some hypnosis for an emotional problem. I had helped them 15 years before, and they knew hypnosis would help them.

Amanda moved me a step closer toward recovery and showed me that the stroke may be a key to what was coming next. Amanda has always been a challenger for me, and I can't tell you how much I appreciate it. For some reason, I feel as if she always raises the bar a little higher. It was a great challenge when she called the year after the stroke and asked if I would consider speaking at the University to a women's group about resilience. Had anyone else asked, I know I would have said no. Amanda never tries to talk me into anything; she just looks at me and asks. This third child of mine is always challenging herself with adventures and physical feats, like a triathlon or a marathon. She has traveled the world, and perhaps I respect this adventurous spirit and want her respect in turn.

The speech shined a bit more hope on my future, and I thought perhaps I was healing and someday just maybe someday...

Essential Oils

Right after the stroke, my friend, Janie, brought me a diffuser and essential oils. I couldn't smell, so I didn't feel it was helping me, but I did use it, because Janie came every day, and I didn't want to seem ungrateful. Years later, I became very interested in essential oils, because more and more research had come out about what they are and how effective they are. You can access over 130 research articles just about essential oils and cancer.

I don't have a medical degree, but I want to share this information. Essential oils have no nutrition, vitamins or minerals. They are chemicals that protect the plant from the threat from viruses, fungus and bacteria.

The use of oils goes back to the most ancient recorded times. We know the Egyptians used them, and they are talked about in the Bible over a thousand times.

There is not a single oil that does only one thing. The Indian Ayurvedic model uses lemons for most everything, because lemons are very plentiful in India. They are used for many things, from nausea to diabetes. And of course, they are used for detoxifying inside and out.

Australians use tea tree, Melaleuca and eucalyptus oil. Here in the states, you see a lot of uses for peppermint. Many oils have similar uses, and perhaps that is so important so that people can find what they need in an oil, grown near where they live.

The most researched oil that I have found is Frankincense oil. The amazing thing about this oil is that it is being studied for its natural cancer treatment. Some of the early research is very interesting in preventing the metastatic growth of cancer in some cases.

When the wise men brought the baby Jesus frankincense and myrrh, those were the main medicines of the day. They rubbed frankincense on babies, because it is believed to support the immune system, while also being an anti-inflammatory agent.

There are many ways to use the oils. Janie had brought me a diffuser, and we know that the area of the brain that deals with smells is right next to the part of our brain (hypothalamus) that deals with memory. In fact, it is estimated that our brain can remember 50,000 scents.

If I go outside early in the spring on a humid morning, I would swear I can smell oranges, and memories of trips to Florida with my family and my Great Aunt flood my senses. The smells of cedar trees remind me of my Dad and bring me peace. I wear that oil often, so often that my granddaughter caught the fragrance in the air and said, "I thought I could smell Ma."

There may be an even bigger reason that we feel peace in the woods. A Japanese scientist has found that there is a group of people that live in an area that is covered with trees. The people that live in this forest area have a very low rate of death from several cancers. Science says that it is because they are inhaling some microbes that are found in nature. These compounds are antifungal and antibacterial, and when you inhale them, it boosts your white blood cells that attack viruses and tumors. Once this hit the news media, the Japanese people created 48 Forest Therapy Trails. Now there is a national past-time to walk along these trails and breathe. This practice is called "forest bathing."

On those days that he could feel spring in the air, my dad would take a deep breath, smile and ask, "Can you smell the angleworms in the air?" Now I realize he was smelling natures microbes, and the serotonin was flooding his brain.

The more that they study nature, the better it gets. Scientists have found another soil microbe that acts like a natural drug for depression and anxiety. It is proving to be as effective as traditional drugs, without all the side effects. You can sniff up these wonderful microbes that lead to the production of serotonin, the happy hormone, just by spending time with a tree. You increase the effect if you are mindful and all your senses get involved. Houseplants can give you phytoncides to breathe, or you can get these amazing anti-fungal, antibacterial compounds from sniffing essential oils like Cyprus or cedar.

All smells are not created equal. There are wonderful smelling lotions that are really synthetic chemicals that are harmful to us. There are three uses of oils: fragrance, food, and therapy. The perfume industry takes a tiny amount and so does the food industry; in fact, a great deal of this is synthetic or created in a lab.

The important part of the essential oils is what they do; the oils flow throughout the plant, carrying nutrition to the cells of the plants and taking the waste products out of the cells. They do many of the same things to our cells. These essential oil cells are so tiny they can even cross the blood brain

barrier. If you put the therapeutic essential oil on the soles of your feet, it will penetrate every cell of your body.

Since our skin is our largest organ in our body, and these very tiny essential oils cells can go throughout our body bringing good things to our cells, why are we not all using them? Maybe because the really good ones are rather pricey. However, it is easier for me to know that something is making me better, than to think about a full page of side effects and drug interactions.

Chapter 7

MY HEALING BELIEF RUNS DEEP

I think for many people it seems strange that I had the audacity to believe I could come up with my own treatment, and that I would think that I could heal with prayer, oils, movement, nature, and I thought worked and what I love. But I had grown up with this belief system. I had heard stories all of my life from my grandmother about her mom and Granny Schaffhauser. Granny S was an old healer woman who cured every illness her family experienced. One of my most treasured heirlooms is a book that belonged to my Great-grandmother Giles and her mother that was published in 1894. The book talks about home remedies and ways to stay healthy.

This is written in the introduction:

"In serious cases of illness the family physician should always be summoned. But remember, nine-tenths of the illnesses that affect mankind can be cured by careful nursing and the applications of simple and safe home remedies, and those that secure the Household Guide will find it ever helpful in giving good counsel in sickness, and a safe guide in health."

Here are a few of the chapter headings in the table of contents:

1. Pure Air
2. Deep Breathing
3. Laughter a Great Tonic
4. Sleep
5. Health in Vegetables and Fruit
6. Plants in the Bedroom
7. Exercise
8. Will Power
9. Happy Thoughts
10. Be Good to Yourself

This spirit of independence did not only come from my oldest grannies either. My grandpa made an onion cough syrup, and I remember my dad making a poultice for a sore on his neck. My kids will remember me making cherry bounce. I never heard anyone talk negative about the medical profession when I was growing up, but rather, they seemed to think doctors were only for emergency situations. I was taught to value good health and to take care of my body.

In our family, there was even an extra belief my mother had, that encouraged good health. When I was about two years old, my brother was born, only to die 8 months later from a very newly diagnosed disease called cystic fibrosis. Those eight months were terror and sadness for my mother. Our whole life changed; because they spent so much time in the hospital, my care was provided by my grandfather who had his own business, a re-tinning shop with big vats of acid that men would dip milk cans into before they were soldered. At three, I started to sit quietly and observe. I went where my grandpa went, sometimes delivering milk cans and sometimes shopping for my great-grandmother. There was always something a small child would like to do or see. I learned unconditional love from my grandfather. I also learned from my mother that we didn't get sick. I am not sure what would have had to happen before she would have taken me to the doctor. I remembered a time I was stung by a bee on my face. I was a young child and my eyes swelled shut. She told me it was time for bed, because it was night time. It was not night time, but I know how fragile my mother was at that time.

This fear she had was so invasive, and I remember when I was about 8 years old and climbing on some cement blocks that were stacked in the backyard, and I fell. A head wound is quite impressive as far as bleeding goes. I tried to wash it off in the outside faucet, but it kept bleeding, so I pushed on it with a towel. Then I decided to ride my bike as fast as I could, thinking the wind would stop the bleeding. It did stop, but I had a small scar on my forehead for many years. That night, without looking at me directly, she said, "Are you okay?" I answered, "Yes," as she smiled and patted my arm. Yes, I think the theory about having seven angels may be true in my case.

My mother was tough about many things. My parents were always remodeling, and she could sew our clothes, knock walls down, and bake bread without question. My dad worked for the power company, so she was home alone with us, doing what needed to be done during the week. Her Achilles heel was illness. I believe she thought she and dad could fix anything. Except illness. My little brother was not talked about, nor was the monster that had the audacity to steal her child. She will say all she wanted to be was a mother, and she was a good mother, but she lived in fear of anything happening to one of us. She believed that if your child went to the hospital, the illness dragon would claim them, because it was the only thing she couldn't fight.

My belief had changed, of course, when I went to nursing school, but that deep belief from my parents is what kept me from being devastated when I was told there was no treatment.

The Mind

I love thoughts and logic. I always have. If I could be a philosopher like in the days of Socrates, it would be my chosen field. I like thinking TOO EXCESS! My father seldom made me angry, but he did when he would look at me and say, "You think too much!" I have been told from friends and teachers to get out of my head. But they don't understand that some people love puzzles and are happy to put huge puzzles together. I like to listen to a story, and then twist and turn each piece of the story puzzle, looking at it until what seemed to be a problem yields its treasure, and the big picture appears.

Books are what I love, and I have loved them since I was a very little girl. I love most genres and especially stories about real people, and what they thought, and how their beliefs created their lives. Two of my favorite presents from Jim were the complete works of Shakespeare for my twenty-fifth birthday and Carl Sandburg's, "Abraham Lincoln," before Becca was born.

One of the most amazing gifts in life, is when we can utilize the talents we have been given for our life's work. I am that blessed. I am a storyteller, a puzzle-master of life stories, and a cheerleader. It is what I have always been and hopefully always will be. I have taken these talents and slapped the word "hypnotist" on what I do. I know many hypnotists that have passed and many that are my peers that do the same thing.

Most the time I don't think of myself as a hypnotist but as a de-hypnotist. We are in hypnosis so often, and our greatest hypnotists are the people and institutions that we love and feel comfortable with. That is what creates our beliefs, which run our lives, and even creates our health and happiness.

I am getting ahead of myself.

What is Hypnosis?

Let me tell you a few things that hypnosis is and is not:

- First, and maybe most important, hypnosis is natural; we all go into it often. Have you ever been reading, daydreaming, doing a project, watching a movie, or playing a videogame, and you weren't even aware of what was going on around you? You were in the zone, that wonderful place where the world stops and your systems can reboot, simply because you were relaxing. Another example is road hypnosis. You see an exit and are surprised when you realize that you are much father that you thought.

- You cannot get stuck in hypnosis. If the hypnotist quit talking, or you decided they were saying something against your beliefs, you would just open your eyes.

- Hypnosis is not sleep. It may look like sleep, and when you open your eyes, you may feel as if you have had a nice rest, but on a MRI you can see that hypnosis and sleep light up two completely different parts of the brain. It is wonderful to use hypnosis as a power nap, because 10 minutes in hypnosis is like a 3-hour nap.

- Hypnosis is not a lie detector or truth serum. You will not tell any secrets; in fact, in most hypnosis sessions, you won't even be asked to talk at all. If you are asked a question, you will answer with an ideomotor response. Before you start, you will be directed to raise one finger for "yes" and a different finger for "no."

- Most importantly, hypnosis is not mind control! It has been portrayed in many movies and books as mind control, starting with du Maurier's book, "Svengali's Web," which was published in 1894. The book became the movie, "Svengali," in 1933 and again in 1955. Sometimes I wish I could snap my fingers and my client could lose the weight they need to lose, let go of a fear, sadness or habits. I wish that magic wand was mine to tap a knee and the pain would be gone. I don't have the wand, and no hypnotist has the power to control your mind.

- The Catholic Church accepted the use of therapeutic hypnosis in 1956, and The American Medical Association accepted it for use with anesthesia in 1958. You will find that medical hypnosis is being used in many ways. Both of the Mayo brothers were hypnotists, and because of the way they used hypnosis during surgery, they were able to use less anesthesia, which resulted in fewer deaths. It was an important reason as to how the Mayo Clinic became so popular in the beginning.

How Does Hypnosis Work?

Hypnosis is focused concentration. When we are relaxed or in a hypnotic state, we respond to suggestion much easier. Again, this is a good/bad situation. The good thing is that if we desire to change our life, we want these suggestions to reboot our subconscious and delete some of those old programs that we have been running that no longer serve us. The bad thing is, this is not an easy thing to do, which in itself is a good/bad scenario.

Our subconscious has protected itself very carefully. Think of a castle with a mote, and that mote is complete with alligators and a draw bridge. If you should get through the mote with all your appendages intact, and are able to climb the castle walls over the sharp pointed edges, you still need to get past the knights that have your best interest at heart and want to protect you by keeping all those beliefs in order. Some of those beliefs have absolutely no truth to them. But imagine that you relax, and you are consciously telling yourself what you want to create in your life. Beautiful, wonderful things that make you strong, healthy, and happy. When that feeling of you, at your best, bathes your cells in pure joy, then you will find that the drawbridge comes down, the alligators sun themselves, and the knights take their afternoon ale break. You may walk into the subconscious and plant new beliefs that work for you.

It reminds me of the story about a new wife that was making a big family dinner. They had purchased a beautiful ham for this first dinner party where both of their parents would be in attendance. Her husband finished his part of the preparations for the dinner and watched her lovingly as she got that ham ready for the oven. His beautiful young wife had made an infusion of pineapple, brown sugar and a secret ingredient that smelled heavenly. Then, she cut tiny lines in the top of the ham and inserted her heavenly concoction and decorated the ham with pieces of pineapple and cherries. It truly was a work of art, and he could imagine his parents being very impressed with his wife's ability. He was surprised when she cut both ends off of the ham. She did the cut with purpose and determination, paying no attention to what it did to the picture she had created. Well this young man was very confused, and he asked his wife why she had cut the ends off the ham. She looked at him in surprise and said, "Why, because you are supposed to. My mother always cuts the ends off the ham." Later in the day as everyone's stomach was full and the conversation was bringing laughter and joy, the young man asked his mother-in-law why she had always cut the ends off the ham before cooking it. The older woman looked at him thoughtfully and said, "Because my mother always did that." The young man's father laughed and said, "I think we will start cutting the ends off our ham, because it was delicious." Now the older mother said, "I am going to call Grandma and see why she cut the ends off the ham; there must be a good reason." Everyone at the table was coming up with logical reasons why the ends were cut off, when the older woman came back to the table laughing and said, "Grandma always cut the ends off the ham, because she didn't have a big enough pan."

How many family beliefs do you have deep inside of you that have nothing to do with you and hold you back from being your best self? When we are born, we have no labels on us, and then immediately we start getting labels slapped on us. Maybe you have been told you never focused on anything, or you always had a temper. Whenever you hear always and never, it is time to question that knight, because who declared such a thing about you? These are only self-fulfilling prophecies. Once you are aware of them, you can choose to not fulfill them anymore.

What do you do with all of these beliefs that are so firmly buried in your subconscious, disguised as absolute truth? You can try to change them with willpower, and you might be able to do that. It is important to remember that willpower is a sprinter, not a long distance runner. You can accomplish what you desire in the short term, but then those old feelings resurface, because the subconscious mind is not on board with the change. As soon as you are not cracking the whip over your willpower and become distracted, your habit is back.

Hypnosis distracts the conscious mind so that gatekeeper steps aside, and the subconscious mind is free to listen to the hypnotist, or yourself if you are doing self-hypnosis. The subconscious is a great friend to you. It only wants you to be happy. The problem is that it does not make decisions in the same way your conscious mind does. Your subconscious mind doesn't understand the negative. "I don't want to get fat," becomes, "I want to get fat." The main way this amazing subconscious creates is through self-talk and emotions. When you declare what you believe over and over, things like: "I will never get out of debt," or, "I will always be overweight, because I take after my mother's family, and they are all overweight," the subconscious, which I am going to call "Spock," will do everything it can to make that happen. It is able to adjust your metabolism, or talk you out of exercise, because it thinks that is what you desire. Self-talk affects your beliefs, and the expectations you have for life. People you love can do the same thing. My first hypnotist was my great-grandfather. He is on my council, and he is the person who helped me when I couldn't balance my ledger. It is strange to me that this man died when I was four years old, and yet I have so many memories of him, and pictures of him touch my heart in a very special way. Perhaps it has to do with the fact that in those very formidable years from two to four, my life was out of a normal rhythm because of my brother's illness and death. Maybe it was because my dad was in "line school" for the power company, and my mother was immersed in illness and sorrow, but that's when my grandparents and great grandparents became my life. Whatever the reasons, my subconscious was very open to their beliefs. It follows completely that when I was growing a wart on my finger, my grandfather was able to remove it using hypnosis.

This is what hypnosis uses to be successful:

1. Desire--I had a desire to be wart free.
2. Trust---I felt safe with letting my grandfather remove my wart.
3. Belief-- I was very sure that my wart would leave

The day came when the wart was going to be removed. We went to the side yard, and my grandfather very carefully placed a long piece of red string across my wart and finger. He told me to stare at the string, and then he placed a penny over the wart. I will never forget any of it, and as a hypnotist, I see it for what it was, a very good induction for a child. He told me to tell the wart to leave, that it was no longer welcome. Then he said I must say, "Go away!" with a very strong voice. He would let the penny go. The wart would be gone soon. I said with a loud voice, "Go away!" and he had been holding my arm with the wart, string and penny on it. When I yelled, he flipped my arm up, sending the penny flying away, and created an instant induction. I was told I could never look for the penny and that the wart would be gone soon; the only thing I needed to do was to believe it happened and think about how beautiful my finger was minus the wart.

I have thought about this often and wonder if he was reading about hypnosis and decided to try it on my wart. It seems like this is most logical, as he read everything. His authors included Emerson, Kant, and Lincoln. He had been to college, and he was both a teacher and an accountant, along with being a musician and a poet. I have heard no stories from anyone else in the family that he performed more hypnosis. With me, he had created enough expectation and belief that my body was able to shut the blood and nutrients off to the wart and remove it.

Let me explain about being a negotiator, because that is what you need to do to create a deal between the conscious mind and the subconscious. I will use someone that wants to quit smoking as an example. Perhaps they have used willpower and quit, and then after a few months, or maybe years, they have just one cigarette and they become a smoker again. Hypnosis can make a deal if a person has a great desire to quit the use of tobacco.

A dialog between conscious and subconscious mind:

Conscious mind - "We are going to quit smoking, because it costs too much and it is bad for our health."

Sub conscious mind - "Are you kidding me? We need to smoke, because it relieves our stress, and stress could kill us."

Conscious mind - "I am very serious; no more cigarettes."

Subconscious mind - "I will bide my time until the first stress comes along."

Then you have a bad day, and you push the angry words down - you smile and think, "I have done everything I can in this situation, and I deserve a cigarette. I want one. I don't have any of these nasty habits that my friends have, and nobody is going to tell me what to do ..."

And then you smoke. But if the hypnotist can change a perception and open the door just a bit, then perhaps the subconscious will discover another healthy, safe way to relieve the stress. For an example, perhaps I see someone that doesn't want people telling them what to do. So, they smoke out of defiance, and I may ask them to imagine a big man sitting behind a cherry wood desk smoking a large cigar. I tell them, "That man is a tobacco executive, and he is laughing at you. Every time you touch a cigarette, or buy a pack of cigarettes, he laughs and states that you are his slave, that you can't stop smoking, that you need to do anything he says about this habit. He says you need to take those little white pieces of paper that are filled with poison and smoke them. The dollars you spend will be for his vacation."

Then, if the person thinks about this and they really don't want anyone to tell them what to do, the subconscious mind works with the conscious mind, and they are unstoppable together.

In my own recovery, there were no emotional blocks to healing. I did not need to negotiate between my conscious and subconscious mind. Everyone was on board. That being said, writing a book about the stroke experience has been full of emotional blocks. Right after I started to heal, doctors and nurses suggested I write a book, and a big part of me thought it was a wonderful idea, but there was, deep in my subconscious mind, a fear. When you have an emotional block, the best thing I have found to do is to tap.

Disease is really just that your body is not at ease, it is in a state of dis-ease.

EFT or Tapping

Emotional freedom technique (EFT), or tapping, is like acupuncture without the needles. Jill and I learned this technique years ago from Tom Masbaum in the Chicago area. Tom's website is EFT-Tom.com. Tom is really a master and is getting great results. Jill is a wonder at asking questions and teaching people to question their feelings. If you have a desire to learn this process and you can't get to Jill or Tom, you can also find resources online with Nick Ortner and his "Tapping Solutions" (TheTappingSolution.com).

Here are the basics of EFT. I assure you that I get amazing results when I use tapping with my hypnosis and coaching clients.

1. Evaluate your discomfort level when you think about the feeling you are struggling with, giving it a rating of 1 - 10. 1 is "it bothers me a little," and 10 is "it is really upsetting."

2. Tap on the endpoints of the meridians. Start with the Karate Chop point. This is the place where you would break a board as a ninja warrior - on the side of your hand, below your little finger. As you tap, say out loud, "Even though I am ____ [angry, sad, lonely, etc.], I deeply and completely love and accept myself." Do this a couple of times.

3. Next, tap on the top of your head a couple of times and say, "This feeling ..." Personally, I then say what I feel like, so I may say, "This feeling of fear makes my stomach hurt ..."

4. Continue to do this at these points:
   A. The top of your head
   B. The eyebrow near the inner eye
   C. The outside of the eye
   D. Under the eye
   E. Under the nose
   F. On the chin
   G. On the collar bone
   H. Under the arm, near where a bra band would be found on a woman

5. Repeat tapping on all of these points

6. Take a deep breath, and evaluate your discomfort level from 1 - 10 again, and I bet it will be less. Keep tapping until you move the number to where you want it to be.

7. I then tap in good stuff like, "Fear reminds me that I am safe. I am loved." Then, I leave off fear and just tap in what

I wish, like, "I am safe - I am loved - the universe has my back - I am a child of God."

8. Take a deep breath and see how you feel

Keep in mind that the body can't decide if something is a real threat or an imagined threat.

Although we can't say exactly why it is that when you tap, it appears to turn off that alarm that the amygdala has to alert us to danger, even if that danger is imaginary. The hippocampus is the part of the brain that plays the "match game" and arranges everything into a category. Does a stubbed toe belong in the same category as a broken heart? The subconscious may think so.

Harvard studies have shown by the use of a MRI and PET, that tapping calms the amygdala down. Cortisol levels decrease 24-50%. David Feinstein PhD., from John Hopkins School of Medicine, says, "The research evidence for energy psychology, coming from a dozen countries suggests that it produces outcomes for a range of conditions that are usually rapid, effective and lasting."

When you are tapping, thoughts and memories can come into your mind that make you wonder where they came from, but those thoughts lead to another and another. You never remove a memory, but you can release the sting or deactivate the button, so that every time a situation, thought or person reminds you subconsciously of that feeling, you don't react without thinking first. Here is a little example. Jill and I ate in cars, especially when we were together. I mean we NEEDED popcorn - lots of popcorn! One time, after riding with us on a long trip, my brother-in-law said in his very direct way that we were rather disgusting. That did nothing to make us stop eating, but it did make us wonder why we did it. Without saying anything to each other, we each tapped when we got home, and the same memory came to both of us. When we were seven- and eleven-years-old, our dad was transferred to a new town about three hours away. When our parents were looking for a house, Mom would pack food, and off we would go. This was in the pre-fast food time you know, covered wagons and all. Well, one Sunday night our food stash was gone, nothing was open, and we had the end of the contents of a peanut butter jar and celery leaves. So we sat in the back seat and spread peanut butter on celery leaves. We were not abused or starving; we were bored, and the clock said it was time to eat. The conscious mind would laugh at such silliness, but the subconscious mind wants us to be safe, so it locked in the *Feeling* of not having the access to food, being mobile in the car, and being hungry. Now we were together, all grown up, and there was a McDonald's on every corner, but our subconscious was still concerned that we should have food when we were in a car. We were both able to release that block by tapping. That was a tiny issue, but people tap on loss, abandonment, fears etc. If we want to heal completely, we have to let go of these things that hold us back. If you don't try to bury those feelings, they will pop up somewhere else, often as pain, anger or depression.

You Can Heal Your Life

Louise Hay has been talking about this since the 1970's in her book, "You can heal your life." In the center of the book, there is a chart that lists physical challenges and the psychological reasons for them. I am always surprised when I look up something I am feeling and find the reason. After the stroke, I read in another book by Louise Hay, "Heal Your Body," Louise's words, "…stroke… giving up… resistance…rather die than change… rejection of life." I was quite angry at Louise, because this was not me! I don't give up, and I am not fearful, and I did not want to die!

It took quite a while for those words stewing and calling out to me, until I was finally brave enough to look at my feelings. We must be brave if we want to heal, and we must be brave if we want an extraordinary life. That being said, it is difficult to look at your real feelings, because it is not always what you project to the world.

My grandmother lived next to us, and she was an amazing woman. If I were to describe her in one word, I would say she was "independent," but she was also intelligent. I remember campaigning for her when she ran for State Treasurer. When she was 97-years-old, she was still reading three papers and plaguing the elected officials with letters. When my grandma was losing her independence, she decided she couldn't drive anymore, so she and her friends could no longer just up and go. She couldn't hear well in crowds, and her greatest fear was that her eyes would get worse, and she wouldn't be able to read. Her friends were dying, and I know she was lonely. At night after I checked on her, I would often say to Jim, "I don't want to get old." He always replied the same way, "Be careful what you wish for, there is only one alternative." With Dad dying at 68, and Becca's surgeries, I was rejecting life in a big way.

This does not mean that my resistance to getting older caused the stroke, but those blocks were very real, and the stronger they get, the more likely they will manifest in some way. I had crazy, deformed arteries, and that is a scientific fact, but I had done many strenuous things, and I never had a problem, until my emotions were experiencing dis-ease or when I was out of harmony, and caused this hopeless feeling.

Muscle Testing

Sometimes we hold onto things for a reason. Often the reason is not even known to our conscious mind. When we want to know what is going on, we can muscle test. Our subconscious mind is like a lie detector. If you put your arm out straight toward the side, and think of something that makes you happy, your arm will be strong. A happy memory makes you strong. Have someone push lightly on your hand, and you will be strong, and the hand will move very little. Now think of something that makes you really sad. Really think about that sad memory, and have someone test you, and you won't be able to keep your arm straight. This is how you can use your body to see what your subconscious is feeling. Ask out loud if you are ready to let go of all the pain, anger or anything else you are holding on to. You may find that you are weak. Then ask if you are ready to let go of some of the pain, and test to see if you are strong. Very often, people are not ready to release all the pain. I know this sounds strange, and it is hard to understand, but our feelings are made to see things as good or bad. Pain seems like something that nobody would want to hang on to, YET the pain brings with it some freedom. After the stroke, nothing was expected of me, and before the stroke, there was much expected. I did not, on a conscious level, want to hang on to anything, especially pain, but on a subconscious level, the freedom from responsibility to anyone or anything, and the lack of expectation, was very nice. For some people, pain can mean you don't have to do something, or you are free to take care of yourself; this is called secondary gain. Be honest with yourself, and ask why you have the pain, or why you do something, over and over, until you get answers. It may be a little question like, "Why do I have such a desire to eat when I am in a car?" or something as big as, "Why am I holding on to this pain after the injury has healed?"

I realized that I could have the freedom from responsibility, if I learned to say, "NO," to the things I did not really want to do and the things that I had outgrown.

I knew that I believed in miracles, and there is a miracle called neuroplasticity. I don't understand why we believed the brain was so different from the body. When we cut ourselves, the white blood cells rush to the scene and repair the damage, and in a short time the cut is healed. Think of what happens when you break a bone. You have it put into alignment, but it is your own body that mends the bones back together. When the brain heals by rewiring an area that has been damaged, it is called "neuroplasticity." That is exactly what I wanted my brain to do.

I believe that if the **"Why"** you want something is big enough, you can do anything. My "why" was very big. My belief system included the idea that I couldn't die until Gina graduated. I knew mothers died; I had friends that died before their children graduated, but for some reason, I couldn't even imagine the very concept. I had not been sick, and perhaps the story would have been different if I had contemplated my own death. As it was, I could use cell memory as part of my healing. Just like when my grandfather had me see my finger minus the wart, I would imagine my brain rewiring itself.

There was a very exciting study that was done in 1981 by Ellen Langer, a Harvard psychologist. For the study, she created an environment that replicated the environment of 1959. The people she chose to study, all in their 70's, all improved their strength, and the average person did 63% better on an intelligence test than they had done on the test before they were in the 1959 environment. When they were surrounded by the magazines, music, TV stations, and even the colors of the appliances from 1959, they evoked cell memory. The more that you can add emotions and feelings to a wonderful memory, the better you can stir the cell memory in a stronger way.

Placebo

I am not talking about a placebo effect, because hypnosis and placebo are different, and they access some different pieces of the brain, yet they also have many similar aspects and access many of the same places in the brain.

Placebo subjects don't need to be hypnotizable, and using a placebo involves deception, because if the subjects understand that they may be getting a sham drug or treatment, it could affect the outcome of the study. This is why it is hard to get clear double blind studies concerning placebos.

To make a placebo or hypnosis work, there has to be expectation. With hypnosis, the person needs to be hypnotizable. The people who are hypnotizable are people who can concentrate. Every "normal" person can be hypnotized. In fact, in the National Guild of Hypnosis we say, "We work with normal people with normal problems." The question is, "Who is normal?" Carl Jung says, "The normal man is a fiction." I tend to believe Rodney Dangerfield when he says, "The only normal people are the ones you don't know too well." Everyone cannot always be hypnotized by the same person, because we all feel comfortable with different people. Because you need to concentrate to be hypnotized, children from infancy to 4-years-old are not your best subjects. Anyone with an IQ under 70 may be questionable, because of the concern for concentration ability. The very best ages for hypnosis, in most situations, are ages 15-21.

We think of hypnosis as being relaxing, and this is a wonderful by-product in many cases, but hypnosis also happens when we are in an emotionally charged situation, and when we are daydreaming.

In some ways, placebos (which means "to please" in Latin) are like hypnosis. Hypnosis may trigger the placebo effect. The placebo effect has been studied since 1700, but it is almost impossible to do scientific studies because of ethics; the person must be told placebos will be used in the study, which may affect the outcome. Here is a study that is an example of the placebo effect: in 2002 Dr. Bruce Moseley, from the College of Medicine at Baylor University, did osteoarthritic knee surgery on 180 patients. They were divided into three groups:

1. They used debridement, removing worn and torn cartilage.
2. Bad cartilage was flushed out in a process called arthroscopic surgery.
3. They simulated surgery (a placebo effect).

After two years, the follow up showed that there was no difference in the outcomes of the three groups; in fact, the simulated surgery showed a better result in the pain management.

The FDA makes every drug pass the placebo effect which is 35%. In other words, 35% of people get better on their own, so a drug must prove that it heals more than 35% of the people that take it. You would be surprised to see the number of drugs that have a success rate that is not much higher than 35% AND have a long list of side effects.

Using brain scans, it has been shown that our brain releases chemicals that mirror the effects of painkillers like morphine. In fact, our brain has better natural drugs than the local pharmacy, because these neurochemicals also have an anti-anxiety effect and help with stress. Hypnosis can tap into these same chemicals that the physicians did in the placebo studies. It has been found that the greatest results come from the symptom-based complaint conditions such as:

1. Chronic pain
2. Mood disorders
3. Insomnia
4. Fatigue
5. Irritable bowel
6. Osteoarthritis
7. Parkinson's Disease

I believe it is wise to follow the words of David Spiegel MD, a psychiatrist at Stanford University, when he said this about hypnosis, "If this were a drug, everyone would be using it."

Hypnosis is a process to change thoughts, beliefs, and actions. It is said that all hypnosis is self-hypnosis, because you are in charge of your mind. If you desire to change something in your life, you are the one that can get your subconscious mind on board, and when that happens, I believe a miracle happens.

Imagination and Visualization

Donald Lynch Jr. MD, from the Eastern Virginia School of Medicine says, "Hypnosis is simply a refined form of applied imagination."

We refine imagination by calling it visualization, but it is really imagining what you want in life, rather than what you don't want. Mark Twain said, "Worry is imagining what you don't want." You can create vision boards with pictures and words of things and feelings that you **Do** desire to create in life. As a hypnotist, I listen to what your dream is, and I help you make a plan. If you are in chronic pain, I make that pain take a step back. If it must remain a constant traveling companion, it is no longer allowed to drive.

Perhaps you can learn like the young airman did after his motorcycle was hit from behind by a car hard enough that his helmet broke in half. He ended up in a body cast, and he would imagine not only that his spine was healing, but that his daughter was melting the pain away with snowballs carefully placed on the heat of the broken vertebrae in his neck. He expected and saw himself running again and being healthier than he was before the accident. He imagined that the doctors were amazed that he had healed so much faster than was expected. He became strong and ran again.

Or maybe you will use your imagination to see yourself removing the fat suit a layer at a time, like peeling an onion, letting go of those old emotions and beliefs that have kept you trapped.

What if you had a dream, since you were a little boy, to be a Navy Seal, and you had worked and worked to make that dream come true? And when you were well into your initial training, you were doing a deep dive, and your eardrum broke so that it was 50% ruptured. Your teammate had the same thing happen, but his was only 10% ruptured. You had one week to heal or you would be rolled out of the program. Could you imagine that your eardrum was healthy and pink, getting stronger and stronger? Could you imagine your dream coming true strong enough that every cell in your body could see you being a Navy Seal? He is a Navy Seal.

Would you believe that an 80-year-old man who had a five-hour shoulder surgery, with complications involving his collarbone, could come out of surgery and only need an over-the-counter analgesic tablet and heal faster due to hypnosis and be pain free? I could tell you 100 more examples I have seen of people using their mind to heal their bodies.

> *"You use hypnosis not as a cure but as a means of*
> *establishing a favorable climate in which to learn."*
> **– Milton H. Erickson**

As a hypnotist, I do not have a magic wand, but if a client listens to me carefully enough and imagines strongly enough, always working to help their body by creating the best environment, they can heal, and I believe miracles can happen.

The Tooth Fairy

We encourage small children to imagine. Parents go to a great amount of trouble to make sure the "Elf On the Shelf" is free to make their children laugh and believe in the magic of Christmas. We have many traditions to encourage imagination in children.

When I was a young mother, I was the Tooth Fairy, and I don't mean for my children. My husband, Jim, was a dentist, and I dressed up in a beautiful, fancy, puffy, white dress, my waist length hair hanging down my back, and went to schools to talk about brushing your teeth. A couple of things I learned from the kids were:

1. You should brush your teeth, because otherwise they will hurt really bad, and the dentist will need to knock them out with a hammer, and there will be a lot of blood.
2. If you have rotten teeth, they all have to come out, and then every night you have to put them in a jar and, one child asked, "Is there any other body piece you can take out and put in a jar, Tooth Fairy?"

3. And when one little girl asked what I did with all the teeth I took, a little boy answered, saying with disbelief at her lack of knowledge, "What do you think dentures are made of?"

I was asked many questions that I was afraid would blow my cover like:

"How do you get into everyone's house, and is that against the law?"

"How come you gave me a quarter and my friend got a dollar?"

"If Amanda is your daughter, does she have to be a tooth fairy when she grows up?" This question started a whole other conversation, because she wanted to be a veterinarian.

My personal favorite was, "Where are your wings?" This was asked at school, and one day I got an answer that almost broke my cover with the desire to explode with uncontrollable laughter. There was a first grader that was mesmerized with my hair. He stood behind me and petted my hair, wrapping his little hands in it, so when his friend asked, "Where are your wings?" before I could take a breath and answer, "At the cleaners," my little friend answered, "I don't know where her wings are, but I can feel her nubs where they attach." There was a rush to feel my shoulder blades.

I also was free to imagine, because many local newspapers ran a story and picture about the tooth fairy that visited schools, one day a big newspaper from Milwaukee called and wanted a story. They would send the photographer up as soon as he returned from a fashion photoshoot in Aspen. I was able to spend some hours as a model, with all the lights and cameras, my giant toothbrush a wand. It was a fun day, and it made me laugh when my cousin in Minnesota saw me when he opened the "Sunday Parade" magazine and saw me, his cousin the Tooth Fairy.

Why do we encourage imagination in small children and then discourage it and talk about reality? Is reality real? Whose reality do you believe? Henry Ford said, "If you think you can or you think you can't, you are right." Both are someone else's reality.

I was told by a young service man that what I am is a Chiropractor for the mind - I give people a thought adjustment. That is the best definition for what I see myself doing. It is called reframing your thoughts. Can you see the blessing, or at least take that big rock in your path that looks like it could be a stumbling block, and turn it into a stepping stone?

Reframing Your Thoughts

We were at Amanda's house in the Bitterroot Mountains. I woke up to the most beautiful morning. When I looked out the bedroom window, I saw the sun shining on the snow on the mountain tops, and the sky was so blue, and I wondered what adventure and joy the day would bring. Then I saw the lake of clouds. I thought about the people who were waking up in Corvallis, not more than a couple of miles away. Those people were waking to a cloudy, dingy morning. Maybe they were considering what they would do before it rained. I took a picture of this sun on the mountain, with the cloud hanging above the town, and sometimes I give it to people to remind them that if the people in the village went out and climbed up the road a short distance, they would find the sunshine again. Remember, the sun is always shinning, because that is what the sun does. We are not always in the right position to see it.

Change your position and reframe your thoughts.

Stages

The stroke took me through many stages. First, I was very brave and determined. I can say at the beginning, when I was in the greatest danger, there was no fear, only faith and a detachment to the outcome. Maybe it had to do with the part of my brain that was affected, but I had experienced this feeling a couple other times in my life. The first time was when I was in labor with Maria, and I heard the conversations about a fear of a uterine rupture, "…hurry… C-section…too far along…" The pain was so intense, that I put all my focused attention on the wall at the bottom of my bed, where there was picture of a cross with Jesus on it with Mary looking up at him. I focused on that picture. Over and over in my mind were the words, "Jesus help me. Mary mother of God help me. Jesus help my baby. Mary mother of God help my baby," over and over. I didn't feel the pain, nor hear anything that would keep me from my work, except when the nurse would shake me and say, "Breathe, you must breathe." I had put myself into a hypnotic trance. I knew nothing about hypnosis at the time, but it worked for me, because it is my natural gift. We forget about what power we have naturally, when we are given a drug to numb our feelings. We can learn from pain and sadness too. I am not suggesting you quit taking any drug your doctor has prescribed. I am suggesting that you develop the skills to let your doctor safely help you remove any drugs you can release.

The other time that is etched in my mind is a day that Becca was so sick, and the doctor thought she had cervical cancer with a growth so big it was pushing on her kidneys. We were rushing her to the hospital, and a calmness came over me. I heard myself in my mind, "The Lord giveth, and the Lord taketh away. Blessed be the name of the Lord." I prayed a prayer of thanksgiving, thanking God for allowing me to have had the great honor of being her mother. I thought of all the joy she had brought to my life, and I was grateful. I slid into that same peace of surrender. When you stop pushing at that mountain in front of you and surrender, sometimes the mountain moves. I write this, yet I can't believe it, because losing a child has to be the worst thing that can happen, and I venture to guess it is the fear of parents everywhere. What I am saying is that sometimes when you are up against the wall and see no way out, let go and surrender to God.

Becca did not have cancer, but months before that she came home with great belly pain, and before we went to the hospital, I told her to imagine a steel box around the pain. My children are masters of imagination. The hospital missed the fact that she was having an appendicitis attack. The appendix burst, but all the poisons stayed in the box she had created. The box was stretching bigger and bigger. After a five-hour surgery, the surgeon came to talk to us and said it was the strangest thing he had ever seen; the appendix was surrounded by a hard capsule keeping the poisons contained. This was integrative medicine at its best. Becca used her imagination, visualization, and hypnosis to protect her body until she could get to a surgeon that could do the surgery. Truly holistic medicine.

Surrender

Possibly the best description I have heard about surrender comes from my friend, David Nelson Ph.D., He is wonderful therapist who uses hypnosis as one of his techniques, but his passion is martial arts. Just like the placebo effect and hypnosis have many similarities but are still different, hypnosis and martial arts have many similarities, yet they are different. One of the similarities is that they are both ways to train the power of your mind, like you would train an energetic puppy into becoming a service dog.

David talks about pain, habits, insomnia etc. as if it is a grizzly bear. You have some options to try and win this fight with the grizzly. You can fight against the bear and tighten all those muscles, but really, do you think you can win against a grizzly? You are just going to be hurt more, which is scientifically true; when your muscles are tight, you hurt more. If you think about something, it will grow. If you constantly think about weight, you seem to attract more weight. If you worry and talk about how you can't sleep, do you really think you will instantly fall into a deep sleep when you lay your head down on that pillow? You could try to outrun the bear, but a grizzly can run 35 miles an hour. I am not sure if that is on a full stomach. What should you do? Quit struggling and don't panic; well, at least try not to panic. Play dead, surrender! Curl into a ball, or lay on your tummy and breathe. Allow this bear of pain, sadness, or fear to just be there as your traveling companion, knowing you will be in control. It may ride along, but it is not the driver. You have the steering wheel.

The second stage I went through with my stroke, was determination. I walked, setting my stick down at the end of each day's walk, only to pick it up the next day and walk at least one more yard.

I was determined to erase the signs of the stroke, so I strapped my arm to a board with my dad's old belt, to keep it from contracting when I slept. One day, when I was at the Neurology Clinic for my weekly check, the doctor had students that were supposed to watch me walk and diagnose my problem. This was a new piece to the puzzle; they were supposed to observe me. I walked for them, and they saw that my right leg was working with my right arm. My left arm should swing as my right leg moved forward. This was almost impossible for me to do. As I practiced on my own, I remembered being a young nursing student working at Children's Hospital in Milwaukee. There was a young girl that had encephalitis, and she was unable to walk. Her parents did everything to get her up walking, but there was a resident that was studying energy and the things we knew about the brain - which was not a lot at that time. The CT, MRI and Pet scans were not being used yet. Doctors began using some of them in the late 1970's and 1980's. The hybrid of the PET fMRI was not being used until 1997.

This connection between the idea of there being two halves of the brain and the way information traveled between them was new and seemed odd. The resident didn't get a great deal of support, except from a nursing student. The young doctor believed that it was very important to crawl before you walked. That was a new idea in the early 1970's, but is understood now.

I was moving in a homo lateral way, which just meant the energy was moving up and down one side of my body at a time, and I was working at 50% efficiency, making it hard to think clearly, have coordination or heal. Maybe I was not healing from anything and just felt exhausted and unmotivated.

When you cross crawl, you activate nerves that go across the corpus callosum, which is the piece that is found between the two halves of your brain. When you do this on a regular basis, you make more neural connections, and the two pieces of your brain work together faster and easier. The cross crawl is very useful for stroke recovery and dyslexia, and for anyone who needs to relearn basic functions.

The cross crawl is like an exaggerated marching in place. To do the cross crawl, raise your right hand above your head as you lift your left knee high. Then do the same for the other side of your body.

About the same time that I was questioning and trying to remember what it was that the young intern had taught me, a woman that I had only met a couple of times called me and asked to come and talk to me. She came and told me about Brain Gym, which is a program created by Gail and Paul Dennison, two psychologists who created an energy program in 1981. This earth angel, who happened into my life, taught me the cross crawl and the lazy 8. To do the lazy 8, you make a figure 8 with your arm and hand, crossing the midline of your body.

In my yoga classes, I do something that triggers the connections between the right and left side of the brain and creates a sense of gratitude. We call it walking the wheel. First, you face the east. The east is symbolic of spring, planting seeds, new projects, and young children. You bend down and gather the blessings, crossing your arms across the midline of your body as you move back to a standing position and pour those blessings over the top of your body. I do this four times. Next, I face the south, the place of growth, the summer of life. Think about the things, people, projects and desires that are growing in your life. Four times you gather the blessings and pour them over your head. Next, face the west or autumn, the time that you harvest the things you have worked to create in life. Gather the blessing, and make sure you cross your midline as you pour those blessings over yourself. Finally, turn to the north, a time of winter, when things are quiet, and you reflect on what you have created and what you wish to plant in your life next spring. It is a time of old age and healing. It too has many blessings to show us!

Although I think the Brain Gym program is great, I have gravitated toward the work of Donna Eden. I think her books can teach you so much, not only about your body, but about how your body affects your mind, and how your mind affects your body.

There is a demonstration of this that seems to never fail. We all know that people who are depressed tend to look down. So during this demonstration, you look down and recite to yourself all the things that are wrong. This is the perfect time to connect to that poor, pitiful Pearl minion and really pour your heart out. Say things like, "I don't think it is fair; I work so hard and can never get ahead," or, "I never have enough money. **Nobody** understands. I have a slow metabolism, and some people just never gain weight - it is not fair! Life's not fair, I need more time, more money, more understanding." See the kind of things that the minion is listening to and shaking her head in agreement? Now look up at the sky and say in your sexiest movie star voice, "Life isn't fair. I need more money, time and understanding." It is very difficult to not laugh, and laughter always raises your mood.

There is a study where electrodes were connected to a people's facial muscles. One set was connected to always keep people frowning and one to always keep people smiling. They were all shown funny movies, and the group of people that were frowning became so depressed they asked to quit the study. You can do your own study by holding a pencil in your teeth which makes you smile, or in your lips, which makes you frown.

Chiropractor

I promised the neurologist two things; one, that I would take a full aspirin every day for the rest of my life and two, that I would protect my neck. He added that means do not go to a chiropractor and let him adjust your neck. Dr. Andrew Weil has written that he does not think there is enough evidence that an adjustment can cause a stroke, but that being said, I ask not to have my neck adjusted. I do believe that having your spine in alignment is very important to your overall health.

My friend Janie, took me to a chiropractor who lives about two hours away who does energy work to adjust a person. I would have a treatment, and at first my arm wouldn't hurt for a week and then later it wouldn't hurt for a month. Soon I was seeing him only as needed. Right before I found this amazing man, my arm was hurting so often that I asked what could be done and was given a prescription for pain medication. When I asked if it would fix my arm, I was told it was nerve pain and the nerves may be firing, which is a good sign, and it may lessen or it may not. The only sure fix would be to cut the nerves. I did not fill the prescription nor consider having my nerves cut.

I did and do go to a chiropractor. I have found a doctor closer to home that also uses standard chiropractic techniques and energy work. Working on your posture is a free and easy. Imagine your head being pulled up to the ceiling or the sky, or walk with a book on your head, or try bending to sit or pick something up off the floor.

Foot Reflexology

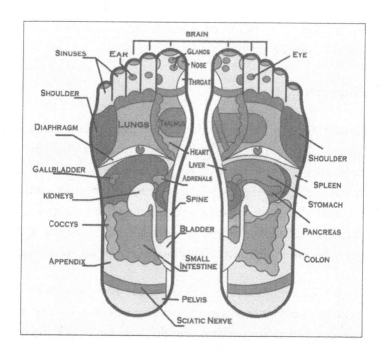

One of my visitors suggested I try foot reflexology. Over the years, I had read a little about this practice, and I felt it was a safe practice to try. My mom gave me a ride to a local practitioner. When she started working on my brain, or the part of the big toe that corresponds to the brain, I didn't think I could stand the pain that shot through my body, and I felt my eyes fill with tears. I asked her to stop, because this was not a deep-massage-kind-of-pain; it was more like a horse-standing-on your-foot-pain. She said it was too early to work on my feet yet, and then she gave me a picture of the foot and suggested I gently work on my toe. From ancient pictures and texts, we know that using the feet for healing was used in China, Japan, India, Russia and Egypt. The belief is that there are energy zones, points and meridians that run through the body, and every organ and body part has a corresponding place on the foot. In the early 1900's, Dr. William Fitzgerald developed the modern zone therapy. You can stimulate more than 7,000 nerves by working with the feet. Some of the things that reflexology has been found to do is:

1. Reduce stress and create relaxation
2. Balance the system
3. Increase energy
4. Improve circulation
5. Increase the immune system
6. Decreases toxins

I have found that it is easy to massage areas of my feet and feel better. I push on areas of my foot, and I am mindful about where I feel it in my body.

Chapter 8

SADNESS

The first step of healing was surrender. Moving ahead bravely, letting go of attachment. The second was determination. But the third step was the next dragon, it was the hardest to face for me. It was fear that manifested as sadness. I have not had a great deal of experience with fear and sadness, and the stroke did not create the fear that was expected, until the winter after the stroke, about six months into the recovery. I was taking a bath, and I started to cry. I thought of tears as a distraction from my determined efforts to heal, and I demanded they stay away. This night I didn't cry, I sobbed, with periods of weeping. In fact, I cried so loud that Jim ran upstairs throwing the bathroom door open as he was reaching for the phone saying, "What's wrong, should I call the ambulance?" I looked at him like I was waking from a dream and said, "I had a stroke," and sobbed more, that kind of sobbing where you are sucking in great amounts of oxygen and your nose is running. You have no control. When I could answer again, I added, "I will never be the same." He looked at me for what seemed a long time and then said, "You did have a stroke and no, you will never be the same. Some things are worse and somethings are better. You are still here, and that is all I care about." He looked at me, and then he left to go back to watch the movie. I quit crying and started to mourn the parts of me that were lost.

We do need a time to mourn and experience the grief that comes from loss. The first of the stages of grief, according to psychologists and grief counselors, is denial. I was putting a positive spin on this and calling it, "faking it until you make it," but it was denial. They are a bit different. The next stage is anger. I did not get very angry, except perhaps at the claw. The third one is bargaining, and I had really bargained with God for those two years until Gina could graduate. Then comes depression, which I was sliding into, and that was followed by acceptance.

We all experience grief of some kind, perhaps it is due to a physical challenge, or maybe it is emotional pain, but don't waste the pain and grief. If you have had the pain of a bad relationship, learn the lessons of the pain. Pain can make you stronger. Maybe you are ready for something new in your life. Birth is painful and messy. Maybe this pain will bring you a bigger life. When I was going through the stroke, I could not see the big picture, but today I am grateful for the stroke, because I grew. You have a few different ways to look at this. You can close up your heart and look for ways to not feel the pain, or you can look at the pain and grief, and see what it is teaching you. Surrender to the lesson, and become stronger. It is very difficult to be stuck in that "between place." It is like being 13. You are no longer a child, but you are also not an adult; you are stuck between what is no more and what is not yet. That is a place we will experience many times in our lives. If you sit with someone who is dying, you watch and they may seem to have already traveled on. They may even talk about people that have died as if they could see them. I believe they have a foot in each world, stuck between what is no longer and what is not yet.

Now the fear came back, and rather than think about getting well, I thought about what would happen if I didn't get well, and what a burden I was and would be to Jim and the girls. I worried that

Maria had skipped a semester and then changed schools to be closer. I worried that this very artistic daughter was being so practical and responsible that she would resent my stealing these years from her. My worst fear was that she would lose her wonderful imagination. I tried to think of things that I wanted, like a chest painted with designs covering it. It comforted me to see her paint. Maria is now the mother of two girls, and she teaches them with imagination and joy.

I thought about how I would never be of service to anyone, because there was so much I couldn't do. I couldn't connect to the Divine or to myself. I sat at the back window, staring out at the snow and wondering what I should do. Every time the mask appeared on my face, I heard my heartbeat in my ears or felt out of breath. I was frozen in fear. Panic was crushing me. Again, I received a great gift.

God comes to us in many ways. If you believe, as I do, that everything is connected, you can see gifts everywhere.

This time, the gift of the angels came in the form of three otters. It wasn't the first time that I saw otters on the lake, and it was always special to see them. Now they stayed where I could watch them, and they made me laugh.

Laughter has many health benefits, from lowering blood pressure, lowering stress hormones, triggering the release of the "feel good endorphins" - a natural pain reliever. It just makes you feel better all over.

In Luke 6:21, laughter is poison to fear. I was in need of some fear poison.

> *"There is nothing in the world so irresistibly*
> *contagious as laughter and good humor."*
> **– Charles Dickens**

I laughed when the otters slid down the snow bank, and when they ate fish like we would eat the corn kernels off a cob of corn. The most amazing thing was, there were times they were by the willow tree closer to the house than I had ever seen them before, and I felt connected to them. Every day, I was fearful that they would be gone. The otters, when they grace us with their presence, only stay a short time, usually a few days or a week at the most. This trio of comedians stayed for two weeks.

Do you believe that everything is connected? I share the Native American belief that animals come to us with a gift or a lesson to share with us. When you see an animal over and over, or you dream about an animal, pay attention! Here are a few of the things that animals share with us, pieces of their personality to remind us of something we are forgetting.

Animals and Nature

Otter - joy, laughter & curiosity	Turtle - love & protection
Wolf - teaching, loyalty & independence	Dove - peace & understanding
Deer - love, gentleness & kindness	Frog - cleansing & introspection
Bear - strength & introspection	Mouse - scrutiny & persistence
Hawk - messenger-be aware of signals	Rabbit - fear
Owl - see the hidden	Spider - create
Squirrel - invest in the future	Ant - purpose
Crane - longevity	Elk - pride & freedom
Horse - strength & stamina	Snake - power
Hummingbird - beauty & wonder	Bat - guardian of the night
Butterfly - transformation	Eagle - Spirit

Being in nature is one way that we can find that moment of peace that refreshes us and gives us the strength to move through the less peaceful parts of life.

Richard Louv coined a new phrase in his 2005 book, "Last Child in the Woods: Saving Our Children from Nature-Deficit Disorder." The phrase is "nature-deficit disorder." It is not a recognized disorder, but in the last thirty years, children have spent less time outdoors, and according to the Institute of Medicine, childhood obesity has doubled for adolescents and tripled in children 6-11 years old. And obesity is not the only symptom of nature-deficit disorder in these children and adolescents. Anxiety, ADHD and depression have also increased at an alarming rate.

It is not only children that are being studied for this idea that nature can work to make people healthier. Landscape designers are working with hospitals and senior centers. Two-thirds of the people the researchers questioned say they would choose to go to a natural setting when they are stressed. 95% of people say they feel better when they can be outside in nature. Researchers say that people allowed to spend even a short time out in nature, demonstrate lower pulse and blood pressure rates, and less muscle tension. The latest of research indicates people who spend time in nature may even live longer. A 2010 study, published in the "Children Youth and Environments Journal," showed that adults who were most dedicated to the environment had grown up with unstructured play in nature. In Europe, there are many "nature play areas," which are areas on public land where kids can build forts and collect rocks. I can feel all the "safety at all costs people" grabbing their chests in a swoon, but what are we losing by orchestrating our children's lives?

My grandma always, no matter the temperature, would open her bedroom window and air out her bedroom. She would walk out on her little porch and breathe deeply, airing out her lungs too.

Nature is one of the best ways to create a positive outlook on life, and that has been proven to make people healthier and more positive, and even live longer.

Using electronic devices and sitting in front of a screen makes you feel isolated. In fact, the College of Cardiology has shown that the amount of screen time you spend increases the likelihood of dying earlier, while people who spend more time outside, live longer and feel a greater connection to everything.

It is easier to feel like you are a part of the web, as if everything matters. Everything is energy, trees and rocks, animals and plants and us. When we feel connected to each other, and believe what we do and how we act affects everyone including ourselves, we have a bigger stake in the game. If we want to follow the law of physics that every action has an equal and opposite reaction, or the law of God that ye shall reap what you plant, both remind us that if we treat other living energy in the web with kindness and love, that is what will be reflected in our life.

Intention

When we are going through a difficult time, or just trying to stay on the path that we have chosen, intention is a powerful tool. I often hear people talk about manifesting their desires, or someone will come to a session with a desire or an intention.

To create change in our life, we must engage our subconscious mind, along with our conscious mind. To do that, you need to use pictures and very specific words. Can you describe what it is you want in your life to a child? If you say, "I want money," you may get a penny or a dollar, or "I want to travel," perhaps a trip to the corner? What does money mean to you? I doubt it means pieces of green paper.

I wanted to be healthy, but what would that word mean to my subconscious mind? I was much healthier than many people. I specifically focused on what I was creating in my life right now, and I focused on all aspects of that one piece of the health I was creating.

In the winter after the stroke, I needed to find happiness and joy. My intention was to find a more positive feeling and to live one day at a time. To manifest my intention, I submerged myself in what I was creating, walking the wheel of mind/body/spirit and emotions/relationships.

When you enter the Peace Corps, you are sent to a school where you are surrounded by people who only speak the language of the country that you are going to, because it is the fastest way to immerse yourself into a different life. It is the same in a military boot camp.

Manifesting or immersing yourself in what you desire, creates 100% focus on that process.

If I was to become happier, I needed to surround myself with things that made me happy. I told myself I would be grateful for how much healing had already happened. Sometimes you must just channel your inner Scarlet O'Hara from "Gone with the Wind," and think, "I will think about that tomorrow."

Our brain will often accept that. You are not judging the thought; you are only dismissing it for a time. It is impossible to not think of a blue elephant. I say, "blue elephant," and you think about it, and no matter how many times you tell yourself not to think of it, it is all you can think of. Remember how your subconscious works; it doesn't understand the negative, and "Don't think about…," becomes, "Think about…"

Remember, stress comes when you are trying to hold two incongruent ideas in your mind at the same time. If you do this and are stressed, you will lose focus. In other words, I could not be happy and think negative thoughts; those are incongruent ideas.

So how do you deal with the negative thoughts that pop into your mind? If you are meditating and this happens, you can imagine that those thoughts float past like clouds, with the promise you will look at them another time.

But when you are experiencing a mind that is just too busy, and negative thoughts are bouncing everywhere, you can replace them with another thought. No matter how advanced your brain is, you can only think of one thing at a time. Your thoughts can flip back and forth, real fast, but still only one at a time. Replace the thought with an affirmation or any other way you can change the focus.

One way I find works is a Buddhist metta meditation:
May I be safe - May I be happy
May I be healthy - May I live in joy
May you be safe - May you be happy
May you be healthy - May you live in joy

You can think about certain people as you recite this, or say it as you drive past cars. I think it is very powerful if you say this for people that have really irritated you. Perhaps we should all be saying this for our government and our politicians.

There is wonderful anecdotal evidence about people healing and situations changing with this little meditation. It changes your brain chemistry if you are frustrated or angry and need to move to kindness.

Talismans

The more emotion you can create around the picture that you imagine, the stronger the focus becomes. I have objects that I carry with me, not because I think of them as magic, but because they remind me that life is magical and miracles are everywhere. A piece of tanned deer hide reminds me to be mindful and stay in the moment. A necklace of amethyst is meant to make me feel less scattered and more focused. If you believe in the healing power of stones, the amethyst works with the brain and helps you to visualize better.

If you have a constant reminder of what your path is, where you are intending to go, and what you are focusing on, you are much more likely to create what it is you want to show up in your life.

Think of the symbolism of the objects, for an example, a blue jay feather symbolizes the warrior. I have a little vase of feathers that I was given that are more valuable to me than a dozen roses. When you focus on the things that have value to you, your RAS (reticular activating system) starts to make you aware of what you want to move forward in your life. I have a picture of Jesus in my stairwell to remind me of gratitude every time I walk down the stairway. All of these things that I have around the house send messages to my RAS that this is the pattern I am looking for; these are the symbols and the seeds I want to plant.

When we are focused on what we really desire, we start to see coincidences or synchronicities. Synchronicity is when your inner mind and your experiences are mirroring each other.

Synchronicity is when you are at the right place at the right time. Those are times when it feels like everything's falling into place.

You can play a little game with your RAS; start by thinking about a color. Any color will do, but really think about it and a number of other things that are also that color. Maybe think about how it is your favorite color, and it just makes you happy to see the color. Sit back and notice how many times you see the color in the next 24 hours. You start to think that your color is everyone's favorite color. It works with anything you want to focus on. Recently, I needed a different car and had a few ideas about what I wanted. I really wanted a Ford Escape, but I was doing research on many different cars. I saw Escapes everywhere I looked, until I decided everyone wanted the same car I wanted.

Perhaps the best thing I did to heal was to become very clear about what it was that that I desired. Then I focused my thoughts and words onto that feeling, so my RAS and synchronicity could apply their magic or what I refer to as "scientific magic."

I talk a lot about focusing on the positive, but it still must feel like what you desire is a possibility. It doesn't have to be a probability but a possibility, or your subconscious will reject it. Then you can trick your subconscious. First, chunk your goal into smaller goals. Let's use weight loss as an example. First, I can tell you from the hypnosis way of thinking, stop trying to lose weight. Remember Yoda, "Do or do not, there is no try." In other words, make up your mind you are going to lose some weight because..." I will not let anyone say, "… because I want to be healthier." It is too vague. I would much rather have someone say, "I am going to look smoking hot in that black dress in my closet," or, "I am going to be able to flex my biceps and feel proud." The reason for saying things like this is because there is more emotion involved.

Being healthy is, of course, the best reason you can find to lose weight, but reframe it in a way you can feel the emotion. Healthy is a word the conscious mind understands, but what would that look like?

There is a great Arabian Proverb, "He who has health, has hope; he who has hope has everything."

I really divided up the healthy part when I was focusing on Becca's wedding and then Gina's high school graduation as an end goal. Did I want to see all the college graduations and weddings? I was not even allowing myself to dream yet about grandchildren. Of course, I wanted all that time, but my subconscious would only allow me to think of that as a small, distant possibility. So start small, and get a success under your belt, and go for the next goal, and then the next, and suddenly you will be your dream.

If you think of walking across the United States, initially it seems impossible. But many people have done just that. Think of the settlers walking west. It didn't stop there. People are walking every year; veterans of wars are walking to draw attention to veterans' issues, and people are walking for attention to raise money for research about health concerns. Alfred Hitchcock, yes the scary movie director, at 19 walked from Long Beach, California to Augusta, Maine (4100 miles) in honor of his parents who died from cancer. Peace Pilgrim crossed the states 7 times in 28 years, walking for both world and individual peace. My personal favorite was Granny D; she walked 3200 miles in 14 months from Los Angeles, California to Washington DC for Campaign Finance reform. She was 90 and had arthritis and emphysema. You can read about her adventure in her book, "Granny D: Walking across America in my 90th year."

I am telling you about these people, because I believe we can do anything we set our minds to do, but not all at one time. These people crossed the United States one step at a time. It didn't matter if they were 19 or 90, they did it one step at a time.

What did matter was that although everyone was making this journey for different reasons, all of them had emotion and a desire to accomplish the goal.

You can model these walkers, whether you want to lose 10 pounds or 100 pounds. Create the feeling of health, imagine your blood pressure at a perfect rate, and then do something every day to make that happen. You can change your blood pressure. Maybe you want to be happier, so you learn to reframe your thoughts and find joyful things to focus on. If a good relationship is your greatest desire, you can become a person you would want to have a relationship with, and then be brave enough to open your heart.

I loved the movie, "The Secret," which took the world by storm some years ago. It taught many people to manifest, but others were frustrated. The problem was that the movie worked very hard to get people to understand that our thoughts are so important to the outcome of our life. They did a wonderful job, but I saw people get frustrated, because there is more work to it than only changing your thoughts. The people that walked across the U.S had to have positive thoughts, or they could not have accomplished such a task. They believed in themselves and the reasons they were walking, but they had to walk.

I healed, and I am very grateful, but I did the work.

Rodeo

A couple of years before the stroke, I was blessed with what I call a setup. To me, a set-up is when we are given an experience that we will need in the future. The question is, will we see it for what it is?

My set-up involved a college that has a rodeo team in Fort Scott, Kansas. I was hired to speak to the bull riders and rodeo clowns about focus. Hypnosis is focused concentration, and self-hypnosis is a powerful tool for these young men.

The reason I know it was a set-up was because it was my first paid speech. I had given many speeches at schools, churches, and local organizations, but the college was flying me to Kansas and paying me $500 to speak. I was the one that would receive the real benefit. That, my friend, was a set-up.

What was it setting me up for? It set me up to see real focus. If we want to change something in our life, we need to know what that something is; now, that seems simple. Simple it is not. Our subconscious mind does not understand that I want to be healthy or happy, or have more money. It does understand something that is full of passion, emotion, and determination, like I want to stay on this 2000-pound twisting beast. Or maybe I want to distract this crazy beast, until the cowboy can get away and escape being stomped on. That, the subconscious can see, touch, and create.

The problem is that we dream tiny dreams, rather than big cowboy visions. I needed a cowboy dream to heal from the stroke. The stroke was a big 2000-pound bull that my 130 pounds was trying to control and tame. I would do it one step at a time just like they learn to be a bull rider one step at a time. I needed laser focus by being sure of what I wanted and feeling the emotions of healing. I needed to feel healthy, not just say I wanted to be healthy.

Sometimes we are like the queen in the Disney movie, "Frozen." We get frightened and freeze our feelings. This happens when we have something happen like a stroke or one of the other five million things that can happen as we walk through life.

If we want to evolve into our best self, we need to be a cowboy or cowgirl. Dream as big as a Montana sky when you are faced with a mountain. Assume you can ride that challenge, and no matter how many times it knocks you off, make up your mind to get back up and ride again.

If you desire to heal from a major hit, whether physical or emotional, you must put as much passion behind your effort as a crazy bull stomping its foot and breathing down your neck would create. When we create what we desire, it is not usually with the determination of a gentle breeze. We must focus and become one with the beast. The cowboy becomes one with the horse or bull, so he can feel the animal's next move and be prepared. You get that from total focus.

I hope I helped those young cowboys create more focus, but I do believe the real purpose of the experience was for my benefit. The Universe was saying, "You need to look at this example of focus, and remember this, because this is a skill you will need. It is a game." How many times do we miss the set-ups that remind us of something we know, or teach us something we are going to need in the future?

Vibrations

The Beach Boys sang, "I'm picking up good vibrations ... Got to keep those loving good vibrations."

> *"We change the world not by what we say or do,*
> *but as a consequence of what we have become.*
> *Thus, every spiritual aspirant serves the world."*
> **– Dr. David Hawkins**

What are vibrations? Everything has energy that vibrates. Some of those things are very dense and vibrate at a slow rate, and some things, like us, vibrate faster. In the 1970's, Dr. John Diamond created Behavior Kinesiology when he found we had indicator muscles that would strengthen or weaken, depending on a positive or negative stimuli. Muscle testing was starting to be studied, and Dr. Diamond started to see the same results over and over. Certain types of music seemed to make people strong or weak; certain types of pictures had similar results.

In 1975, Dr. David Hawkins, a well-known psychiatrist and physician, started researching kinesiological response to truth and lies. For over twenty years, he tested the full range of emotions of the human consciousness. He created a scale of sorts in his book, "Power vs. Force." Dr. Hawkins' scale rated emotions from Shame at 20 to Enlightenment from 700 – 1000. However, many other energy teachers have created vibrational scales. I give you eight levels and a combination of words that describe each level. The first four levels are slow vibrations, and they take more energy than they give. In the top four levels, the vibration is faster and people are creating a better world. When we can stay in the top four levels, we move from being a victim to taking back our own power. We can raise the vibrations of everyone around us, because we affect other people who are within ten feet of us. The higher our vibration, the stronger the effect of the energy that surrounds us. Maybe you have been in a group when someone came in with such a negative attitude that you felt the lights dim; that was a person with such a low vibration that they have become an energy vampire. There are other people that can be, as the song goes, "sunshine on a cloudy day." These positive people are on the high end of the vibrational scale.

1. Words that describe the lowest level of vibrations are: fear, shame, victimhood, despising, miserable, humiliation, dirty, disgusting, disgraceful, guilt, victim, illness, rage, vindictive, evil, blame, destruction, and anxiety.

2. The second level is described in words like: apathy, despair, hopelessness and depression. You have a lack of both resources and energy, feel heavy, and you just don't care. People here may be sad and feel a loss, and are dependent. They accept failure, are often tragic and friendless, and they have regrets and withdraw from life.

3. Third level people return to feeling, but those feeling are still low vibrations, like jealousy and insecurity. They may still reject life and be obsessive and filled with worry. They may find themselves paranoid, angry, and filled with hatred and they may seek revenge.

4. We are moving up the ladder, and this step is filled with both desire and denial. People at this level often find themselves disappointed, craving, addictive, and obsessed with the

idea of more. They are often described as greedy, prideful, arrogant, defensive, worried, and discouraged. When you are at this level, you may find yourself filled with doubt and blame, and you may be pessimistic, bored and impatient. This is the dividing line or the turning point. People below this level see themselves as victims; people above this level take back their personal power.

5. The words that describe people at this level are trusting, optimistic, contented, hopeful, courageous, and open-minded; they have high self-esteem, empathy, and sympathy. These people are accepting, and this is where major transformation happens.

6. People at the sixth level are emotionally calm. They are free of discrimination, and they are not interested in who is right or wrong. At this level, you can make a deal between the subconscious and conscious mind to change negative behavior. These people are self-disciplined, enthusiastic, and have positive expectations and are happy.

7. At the seventh level, people are filled with unconditional love, and unchanging joy has become a way of life. It is where people deal with everything in a loving way, and they feel everything is connected to everything, and everything is alive and of value. This is the level of true happiness and healing; the beauty and perfection of creation becomes effortless, and people at this level see good everywhere and connect to peace.

8. Enlightenment influences all of mankind at this level. It is the level of the greatest teachers and leaders. Dr. Hawkins would rate this level at 700 – 1000. Jesus would be at 1000.

One person at level 5 would affect the energy of 400,000 people below the turning point.

One person at level 6 affects the energy of 750,000 people below the turning point.

One person at level 7 affects the energy of 10 million people below the turning point.

One person at level 8 affect the energy of 70 million people below the turning point.

Dr. Hawkins says, as of 1995, the collective consciousness jumped to 207, or past the turning point. Dr. Hawkins says we can raise our vibrations by first deciding where we are on the scale, and then where we want to be. Find the masters that are at that next level and read their teachings and model their behavior. When you raise your vibration, you affect everyone that is in your geographical area. Think of all the good people we have working toward peace, love, and joy on earth right now.

What would happen to the earth and the vibrations, if more people joined the group called Optimist International? What an amazing group of humans that are working to make the world better. What if those of us who choose not to join the group would just read the Optimist Creed every day, using it like an affirmation? Here are a few of my favorite affirmation lines from this amazing creed:

Promise yourself:

To be so strong that nothing can disturb your peace of mind.

To think only of the best, to work only for the best, and to expect only the best.

To be as enthusiastic about the success of others as you are about your own.

To forget the mistakes of the past and press on to the greater achievements of the future.

To give so much time to the improvement of yourself that you have no time to criticize others.

To be too large for worry, too noble for anger, too strong for fear, and too happy to permit the presence of trouble.
– Optimist International

This is really something to aspire to. I truly believe that the world is changing, and our reality will depend on the vibrations of the people on the planet. We hear about all the people that cause pain, but there are so many more groups of ordinary people like you and me who are holding a higher expectation for the future.

If you watch the evening news and feel fear about the world's situation, remember the very wise words of Mahatma Gandhi:

"When I despair, I remember that through history, the way of truth and love has always won. There have been tyrants and murderers, and for a time they can seem invincible, but in the end, they always fall. Think of it - always."

The Arts

One of the things that makes life worth living is the arts. I come from a family of artists. My mother painted with flowers. Her gardens were something to see, each flower coaxed to be its best. She talked to them and loved them, especially her roses. My dad could draw, sculpt and carve. Jill and Patrick have inherited his talents and made them grow in their own ways. The pictures I have included in this book are theirs. Someone asked why I wanted to include drawings, and the reason is that they are pretty and make me happy. I hope anyone that reads this book will feel the gift of the drawings.

Right after the stroke, I was gifted with a beautiful picture book of all the mythical goddesses. Each picture describes a facet of the personality of "woman." My friend told me that each of us has a piece of the mythical goddess inside. I would sit with this big coffee table book and page through it, studying the pictures of these beautiful woman from every culture.

Bast, a goddess from Egypt, protects pregnant women and children

Athena, a Greek goddess that was so wise she could see the truth of every situation.

Artemis had a strong independent spirit and was strong in her body.

Celtic Cerridwen watches over nature and farmers.

I wondered how the world would be different if we made each child feel special. We no longer teach mythology, but what if we realized each child was as unique as the colors of autumn leaves.

That thought always makes me think of a story I heard once about a king that was unhappy with the way children were being treated in his kingdom. The king and queen came up with a plan to remedy the problem that was causing them distress. The queen had twin babies, and one month after the birth of the prince and the princess, the king called a meeting of all the villagers. What he said was meant to shock them. He achieved his goal and then some. Here is what he told the villagers: "There were many children born in this village this month, along with the Prince and the Princess. In the night when you were asleep, I took two of your children and exchanged them with my own children. I will expect my children to be treated as they should be treated, and when the children are 18, I will announce who the real princess and prince are in the kingdom. Until then, I will be watching the children grow. The people were shocked, and they looked at the new babies with great interest. Everyone started to treat each child as a royal baby. The children were taught self-discipline as the king would teach his children. They were kept clean and made to laugh and learn. After eighteen years, the village was very different. Now there were schools and stories. Laughter filled the streets, and people had grown kind to one another. The month came that the babies had been born, and again all the people of the kingdom came together to hear what the king had to say. Everyone was guessing who was the real prince and princess. The king listened to all the speculations and then announced they were right, each of them was right. All children were special, unique princesses and princes. The king announced that he had never let his children out of his reach, and each child had been raised in its respective family.

I agree with this story, but I think we, at times, make mistakes when we tell girls they are princesses, because we act as if a princess needs to be rescued by Prince Charming, or that they need to live in huge houses and wear expensive clothes. What if we taught mythology, and each child was taught that they are the beloved child of God, each a princess or prince of heaven? What if they learned that like Gaia, it was admirable to take care of the earth? I would sit and look at the pictures and wonder.

Art therapy has been around for a long time, and often it is easier to draw your sadness than to speak the words.

It has been discovered that mindlessly doodling for 10 minutes affects the brain like meditating. Now adults are starting to color and find the relaxation it brings. It is hypnotic, because your conscious mind moves aside, too busy deciding the color to use, and the subconscious rests as it creates.

Jim and I went to Italy to visit his family and explore. Two things happened to me in Florence. The first thing happened when we went to see Michelangelo's David. The 14-foot gleaming white marble statue seemed alive with all the beauty that a body could possess. I like art and appreciated it as much as most people, but at that moment, when I thought of someone being able to make marble come to life, it was overwhelming. I saw people with tears in their eyes, as they just stood and looked at the beauty. I have heard that when people asked Michelangelo how he could create such a thing of beauty, he said, "David was always in the marble, I just had to chip away the excess." Michelangelo was 26 years old and worked for two years, sleeping very little, and when he did sleep for a couple hours, it was usually with his clothes and boots on.

Music is another art that can touch our soul. Music, like art, is everywhere - in the sounds of the birds chirping, the water running, and the wind dancing in the trees. There are people that have the talent to be able to create music, whether with an instrument or using their voice as an instrument.

There are songs that can make us happy, no matter the mood we are experiencing at the time. But a song can also make us remember a feeling and take us back to the moment something significant happened in our life. We can also be somewhere, and that place will trigger a memory of a song. That song can become an earworm; that song that gets stuck in your head. Researchers say that 92% of people have this earworm experience about once a week.

Music can make us heal by balancing our hormones and releasing endorphins – those feel-good neurochemicals that reduce chronic pain and depression and bring us peace. Sometimes a song can make us feel powerful and determined like the song, "Eye of the Tiger," by the band Survivor. I feel my determination grow when I hear the "Rocky" theme song.

Longfellow wrote that music is the universal language.

I think most people have a favorite genre of music, that little playlist in our head. I like country or folk music, because I like the storytelling of it. I can't understand rap music, but the beat of it makes my body move. The beat touches each of us in a different way, depending on our vibration frequency. Some music makes you have happy feet and some make you cry.

The one type of music I had no feelings for was the sound of the sopranos in opera, until one day when we were in Florence and we came around a corner, and there on the street, the most beautiful sound I had ever heard was coming from a girl singing soprano opera. She was using her whole body to sing her song. I could not understand a word of her song, but it touched my heart.

After the stroke, the music that helped me heal came from two folk singers that I met at the National Wellness Conference, Jana Stanfield and David Roth.

A song that helped me through many a hard day is called, "Butterfly." You can hear Jana Stanfield on YouTube, and I suggest you include "Butterfly" on your playlist.

The song is about a girl that is overwhelmed. She sees a caterpillar and thinks how much they are like. I think anyone that has gone through a big change has felt like this caterpillar and can understand her conversation with the butterfly.

She said...

Butterfly, please tell me again it's going to be alright.
I can feel a change is coming
I can feel it in my skin
I can feel myself outgrowing this life I've been living in
And I'm afraid, afraid of change
Butterfly, please tell me again I'm going to be alright

Tattoo

Two years after the stroke, Gina was leaving for college. I was much better, but I was still doing hypnosis now and then. I was frightened and confused about my next best step.

I entered a new stage where I was frightened about the future. If there is one emotion I dislike, it is fear. I think there are really only two emotions - fear and love. All emotions fall into one category or the other. It felt like I was afraid of everything. The further I moved away from the stroke, the more I feared the dragon. I was afraid something would happen to Jim. I was afraid something would happen to one of the girls. I was afraid we would go bankrupt, because the stroke had devastated our finances. You name it, I was bordering on panic about it. I knew what I had been fighting for when I had been face to face with the Dragon Stroke, but now it felt like I was fighting a mist. As soon as I turned toward it, it was gone, and I would see the smoky form dart around the corner, or I would feel it standing behind me again.

I needed to find tools to help me. This is when I decided to move forward. I needed a banner or something that would remind me that I was brave. The Gage family crest motto is, "courage without fear." I needed a constant reminder, and it better be tattooed on me to remember it. Then Gina came to me and said now that she was 18, she was getting a tattoo, and did I want to get one too?

14% of all Americans have a tattoo. 40% of people 26-40 have a tattoo. I knew exactly two people that were older than 40 that had a tattoo; my uncle, who wore a long sleeved shirt to hide the tattoo that he felt was a mistake, and an older woman that had a flower on her breast which she did not hide, but the flower was affected by gravity, and didn't look like it did on the day it was created.

Standing naked in front of the mirror, I tried to decide what would not sag as I aged. My big toe was a pretty safe bet. I became one of the 43% of tattooed people that think the meaning of the tattoo is the most important. I decided to have a blue butterfly on my big toe. I could look down at my foot whenever I was frightened and remember that I may still be a caterpillar, but I was transforming. Of course that dark cocoon is scary, but I was going to FLY!

Shane Wallin, of Minneapolis and San Diego, is a tattoo artist who started working with women post-mastectomy by creating beautiful pictures on their wound sites. The first woman that asked for help was beautiful, and he created a black lace bra for her. He created flowers for another woman. Some of the artists create nipples and areolas. Women can look at beauty, rather than what feels like destruction.

Maybe that is why sailors and soldiers were the first people to get tattoos and still are. My nephews, who are in the military, have very brave and meaningful artwork decorating the canvas of their skin. Gina has more than one tattoo, and they are all meaningful, like the bee tattoo that she got after her stint with cancer. The bee is a symbol of success in the face of impossibility.

I am not saying that I have never been afraid since the day I left the tattoo parlor, but I will tell you, for me, I feel more courageous. My butterfly reminds me of who I am and who I am becoming.

Aging

On the subject of aging, I was doing much better, but still not where I wanted to be. I was about to make the transition from parenthood to...what? I think many people go through what society calls a "midlife crisis" or the "change" - and not just women either.

This is a time when we decide how we are going to choose to age and think about aging.

Louise Hay says, in her book, "You can heal your Body," that aging is also a thinking problem that involves:

1. Social beliefs
2. Old thinking

3. Fear of being yourself
4. Rejection of the now

Could it be that our problems with aging are a result of "stinkin' thinkin'?"

Every day after the stroke, my grandma would say, "Now you understand what it feels like to be old." She was right, I felt fatigue, and I felt I lost the freedom to jump in the car and go where I wanted to go. My memory, strength, hearing, eyes, sense of taste and sense of smell had all failed me. I think it is hard to explain to someone what it feels like if you have never had a sense that your body has betrayed you. All the times that I feared old age and said I didn't want to grow old were coming to haunt me. What did I believe? What is aging, and how was it going to look in my life?

When we take our first breath, we start to die. Our cells are constantly changing, dying and being reborn. The cells of our stomach lining reproduce every three to four days, red blood cells in 4 months, white cells in more than a year, skin cells in two to three weeks and colon cells every four days.

It is the subconscious mind that tells us who we are, unless we consciously question those beliefs and make a choice. It is that mama cell telling the baby cell, "This is who we are. Jane has had a stroke. This is what we believe a person that has had a stroke is like."

Bruce Lipton, the wonderful genetic scientist who wrote, "The Biology of Belief," found that you could take two cells from different parts of the body, for example, a liver cell and a bone cell, and put the same chemical medium on them in the petri dish, and the one cell will change to become like the other one. Bruce Lipton says that we are all like waking petri dishes, and our thoughts are the neuro-chemicals that are like the medium that bathes these cells and changes them.

One thing I am very sure about is that I don't want to end up like the man in this story:

A man named Joe died and went to heaven. St. Peter met him and said, "Welcome to heaven Joe, come with me, and we will get you settled in." Well, Joe followed St. Peter, with his long white beard that seemed to glow, so it was easy to follow him. There were angels everywhere carry boxes and laughing. Finally, Joe had to ask, "St. Peter, what are the angels doing? I see rooms that are lit up, and the angels seem so happy carrying those boxes and pushing them down the chute. And I see rooms with the doors closed. I don't understand." But Joe felt happy, because the angels were so happy. If you know anything about angels at all, you know that when an angel is happy, everyone is happy; it is rather contagious, like joy always is.

Just then, Joe saw a door with his name on it and he stopped. He was so excited. "St. Peter is this my room?"

"It is Joe," St. Peter said rather sadly.

"I want to go in, please." No matter how St. Peter tried to get Joe to move on, he was adamant that he go into the room.

When the door was opened, Joe looked around in disbelief.

"What is this? Why is my room full of boxes?"

"Joe each box is full of life - experiences, blessings, joys, mistakes and sorrow. You were so afraid of making a mistake, or being hurt that you always did what you did the day before. You never asked for the boxes, and they were never sent."

I don't know the answers to life, but I do want to open the boxes, and one thing I have learned through all the things that happened in my life is, life is precious. I will never see this moment again.

Maybe it is easier when you have a life or death experience to remember that there is not a promise that you or a loved one will be here tomorrow.

I like the song, "Live Like You Were Dying," by Tim Nichols and Craig Wiseman. Tim McGraw sang it, and it is about a man who was told he had cancer, and someone asked him what he did when he got such bad news.

The lyrics of the chorus are as follows:

I went sky divin'
I went rocky mountain climbin'
I went 2.7 seconds on a bull named Fu Manchu.
And I loved deeper,
And I spoke sweeter,
And I gave forgiveness I've been denying,
And he said someday I hope you get the chance,
To live like you were dyin'.

Personally, I hope you don't go through a life-changing trauma, but I do wish everyone would understand we are not guaranteed a length of time here on earth.

According to the Organization for Economic Cooperation and Development (OECD), men in the U.S. are expected to live to 76 years and women 81 years, or an average of 78.7 years. That makes the United States 26th in longevity, out of 36 members. The United Kingdom has an average longevity of 81 years, and Switzerland is first at 82.8years; Russia is last at 69.8 years. The United States increased 9 years in longevity between 1960 and 2011, but that was the lowest rate of improvement out of the 36 countries. Japan had the highest rate of improvement and increased 15 years. Perhaps the problem is that our obesity rate was 15% in 1978, and today it is 36.5%.

We spend 17.7 % of our GDP on healthcare - more than any other country. We spend $8,508 per capita in comparison to $3,339in the other countries.

This is not a guarantee that you will live this long; it is only a guess. There is another way to put this into perspective. Take the age of your oldest relative (they do not need to be living now, but take the one who lived the longest) or take the national average for your sex. Now subtract the age you are right now. For example, my grandmother lived to age 98, and I am 63. 98 – 63 = 35 years. If I live to my grandma's age, I have 35 years left. Am I living the way I want to live for 35 more years? If I wanted to reframe what 35 years looks like, that is approximately the time between my age of 30 and now. There has been a lot of life that has happened to me between when I was 30 and 63!

How Do You Want to Be Remembered?

The best advice I ever got on this subject came from my Dad when I was eighteen and ready to leave for nursing school. Dad told me that I needed to live my life so I could feel good about myself and my decisions. He took a worn piece of folded paper from his wallet and gave it to me. It was a poem called, "The Man in the Mirror," and these were the words that I would share with any young person.

ANON

For it isn't your Father, or Mother, or Wife,
Whose judgement upon you must pass.
The fellow whose verdict counts most in your life
You can fool the whole world down the pathway of years,
And get pats on the back as you pass,
But your final reward will be heartache and tears,
If you've cheated the man in the glass.

At the beginning of this path I found myself on, I was far from sure that I would be able to win the battle with this dragon. So I decided to focus on how I wanted the people I loved to remember me. I wanted them to remember me as strong and funny. I wanted them to think of me having loved life, and most of all, loved them with all my heart. The human mind tends to remember the last thing that happened, so it made sense to me that what I did now would be what they remembered. The big thing was that I needed to be my best self, because I needed to look myself in the mirror.

Here I am, seventeen years later and still wondering what legacy I will leave. I have been truly blessed with good parents and siblings that are also my friends. I am still in love with the same man, and not only do we have four of the most amazing daughters, but now we have four men of good and strong character to be our sons. And a blessing I never expected to see - eight wonderful grandchildren! There has been sadness and disappointment in some of the life boxes I opened, but the blessings completely outweigh the sadness. I know my immediate and extended family, and my friends, are my blessings in this life.

The Bible says, "To whom much is given, much is expected."

A wise older Native American man and I were having a discussion, when he said to remember we were the Elders now, and there was a great responsibility that came with it. I started to think about my responsibility to life, to my legacy.

I think each of us has something to bring to life that will make the web more beautiful and stronger. Maybe our responsibility is to just leave the world a bit better than it was when we came.

I love the old saying by Ralph Waldo Emerson, "When you were born you were crying and everyone else was smiling. Live your life so at the end, you're the one who is smiling and everyone else is crying."

In Conclusion

After seventeen years, this is my balance sheet today:

- Agnosis - My sense of smell and taste are both functioning, but I have lost a great deal of hearing, especially in my right ear. I still have trouble keeping people's faces and names together, but I can remember every story they have told me.
- Amnesia -There are still pieces of my life and memories I have no access to. These memories are found in the part of my brain that hold the memories of the girls growing up. The good news is that every now and then I get a flash of a memory, and I think the memories are starting to wake up after years in a coma.
- Aphasia - I think words come out right most of the time. What happened as I was healing was that I became so used to creating words that sometimes I am afraid I speak "Seuss," as in Dr. Seuss.

- Anosognosia - I don't deny a disability anymore; I look any disability straight in the face and ask, "I wonder what else is possible?"
- Somatoparaphrenia - The claw is trained for the most part; every now and then my right hand will still throw something.
- Diplopia - At my last eye exam, the optometrist decided I could try a prescription without the prisms.
- Horner's syndrome - My face mask only shows up if I take a very hot bath. My pupils are not completely equal, and I am the most comfortable with sunglasses, but I feel this is not very far from normal.
- All the other challenges I had at the beginning have melted away. My energy level is higher than it ever was before the stroke.

I have not had all the brain tests available, because they are so expensive, and there is nothing to accomplish by having the tests since there is no treatment. However, the doctors estimate by listening with a stethoscope that the right carotid artery is open and the left one is at least 60% open.

The blessing in this very rocky path was that I decided what I believe.

I Believe:

1. Love is everything. Not just loving the people that are in our family, but loving life, nature and all the wonder. What would happen if you weren't afraid to take a chance? What if you said, "Yes," to life like in the Jim Carrey movie, "Yes Man"? The character is bored with life, frustrated and angry, and he goes to a self-help seminar where he is instructed to

say, "Yes," to every opportunity that comes his way. He, of course, goes overboard, but it changes his life. There is a very sad thought in this quote from Henry David Thoreau in "Civil"- "Most men lead lives of quiet desperation and go to the grave with the song still in them." I promise you that if you live in wonder, rather than fear, your life will become new and exciting. It would take me a whole book to tell you the wonderful stories I have just because I say, "Yes," to life.

2. There are things in life that could easily be labeled as bad deals, unfair, unjust, not understandable, just nasty crapola. More than any other time, you need faith at this time. This is the time to believe God, the Universe, or whatever you call this amazing, loving life force that Jesus and all the great teachers have talked about, has got your back. Granted, at those times the Great One is not sharing with you the big picture. This is the time to borrow my "BIG MEDICINE" poem:

When you come to the edge of all the light you've known,
And are about to step off into the darkness of the unknown,
Faith is knowing one of two things will happen, there will
Be something solid to stand on or you will be taught how to fly

3. When you come to the time that you have a great desire to change something in your life, it is also the time to picture what it is you desire. Practice until you can see the life that is yours in as many vivid details as you can imagine. Remember, your subconscious does not know if something is real or imagined. See it, and then be grateful for that vivid, interesting, abundant life that is yours, and it will be on its way to you in some form, so watch for the signs. Make up wonder songs full of gratitude. If you are tempted to think

of the reasons why this amazing life can't be yours, think of yourself as a racehorse, and put those blinders on.

4. Don't get caught up in the boiled frog syndrome. The boiled frog syndrome is the theory that if you put a frog in boiling water, it will jump out, but if you put a frog in water and slowly turn up the heat, it will cook. We are constantly allowing stress and other situations that slowly cook us. Perhaps we develop an autoimmune disease, or depression, or have a heart attack or go through a divorce. Stress kills, or it can make you a stronger, more resilient person with self-esteem and a strong immune system.

5. Remember God is Love, and we are told the most important commandment is to love God with everything we have got, and to love our neighbor as ourselves. This means we have to love the amazing one-of-a-kind person that we are. They literally broke the mold after each of us were born.

These are some of the beliefs I find helpful on the path I am choosing to travel. May each of you follow your path bravely with love, faith and joy!

ABOUT THE AUTHOR

Jane Govoni is happy to be a wife, mother and grandmother. She is the owner of Sky Blue Dreams. She is a board certified consulting hypnotist/coach, an instructor for both the National Guild of Hypnotists and the International Hypnosis Federation, and she is a speaker and an author.

You can find her in Oxford, Wisconsin on a little lake with her husband Jim and Daisy the dog.

Contact Jane through www.janegovoni.com, jane@skybluedreams.net, www.skybluedreams.net, on Facebook or Twitter, or follow her blog.

ACKNOWLEDGEMENTS

I thank God for giving me those two years...plus another 15!

I would like to thank Jim and our girls, Becca, Maria, Amanda and Gina, for standing by me and making me feel that I was enough at each stage. I would like to thank my boys Eric, Ron, Aaron and Adam for being so loving to me. You make me never regret not having boys, because you have filled that place in my heart. Bella, Hudson, Milana, Willow, Hazel, Coulter, Maceo and Wyatt, thank you for being a big reason I want to live to 100 years old!

I want to thank my Mom, Nancy Gage for teaching me gratitude and the importance of health.

To my siblings, I will never be able to tell you what you mean to me. Each of you had your own way to help me heal and find joy. Thank you Dan Govoni, Jill and Ken Bachmann, Mike and Amy Gage, Patrick Gage, Kate and Tom Finco, and John Gage.

To my nieces and nephews including the "greats," and my cousins, I am so blessed to have you in my life.

A special thanks to Jill and Pat for the pictures. Jill is more than a sibling; she is also a business partner. I want to thank my friends, Roxy Larson for being my friend for the last 38 years through it all, and my new friends, like Carol Schilling and my yoga ladies, that have listened to me as I wrote the book.

Thank you, Elizabeth Phillps, for keeping everything at the clinic moving smoothly and for keeping Jim stable through the crisis. And thank you, Heather Larson, for doing some of my work so I could write.

I thank all my Earth Angels from my town who corrected my errors at the bank, brought food, encouragement, kindness and helped me heal, because they accepted me broken.

I especially want to thank Marcia Tank, John Zimmer, and Karyn niin Kitigade, who are responsible for putting in commas and making it clear from my thoughts to where you can understand my thoughts!

And of course a great thanks to the Hay House Balboa team.